Hello Gorgeous

Empowering Wisdom from Bold Women to Inspire Greatness

Lola Sánchez Herrero and Ana Sánchez-Gal

Founders of The Oliver Gal Artist Co.

ROCK
POINT

To all the women in our family.
To Mom, our sisters, our nieces, and our dear cousin.
You are the reason that we do what we do.
To Dad, for raising us to be our most authentic,
fearless, and fierce selves.

— Lola and Ana

CONTENTS

INTRODUCTION

Oliver Gal Artist Co. is a growing art and lifestyle brand in South Florida, spearheaded by us, sisters and artists, Lola Sánchez Herrero and Ana Sánchez-Gal. We created Oliver Gal to capture life's most haute moments, avant-garde objects, and splendid lifestyles in art and other products. Our company has become a worldwide phenomenon, with thousands of collectors and followers who see and buy our artwork and lifestyle products to express themselves and complement the décor of their homes. Now, we travel the world participating in award shows and signing events from Miami to Tokyo.

We were concocting this incredible venture in our minds long before it became a reality. As sisters, we've always been very close, and we've always helped each other to grow, to develop our wildest ambitions. Our love for creativity is something we share, alongside a relentless passion for doing things in a different way, **to walk the undiscovered path—always hand in hand**.

We always thought about bringing haute art to the people. Art that evolves in a fashion-like motion, while keeping the highest-quality materials and creations. However, we've been open to the public since 2012. Our collective houses several artists, creating a convergence of different artistic visions that evolves with each project. **Our inspiration is life itself**. We believe art should reflect who you are, what you look up to, and where you see yourself, while complementing the space you want to unwind in or create at.

Each of our art pieces is the result of creative and ingenious research. We strive to follow not only fashion trends but also worldwide events and happenings. We believe in art that evolves with the times, is in constant change, and reflects your personality at every stage of your life. By doing this we have gathered a following that continues to inspire us and constantly encourage us to come up with new ideas so that we remain trendsetters instead of followers.

We have worked very hard and have faced many setbacks in order to get to where we are now. While people may see us as successful entrepreneurs or "two very lucky women," we see the many challenges we encountered along the way, not only as immigrants to a new country and newcomers to an aging industry, but also as tough workers.

Being an entrepreneur is not an easy task; it is a daunting mountain that must be climbed every day. To top that off, we are mothers, sisters, daughters, employees, bosses, and many other roles that must also be attended to. It is because of this that we took the chance to write a book to inspire and move others, to remind us, women, that we are incredibly fierce and powerful and that the world is ready to see us unleash our potential and will receive us with gratitude.

Through these pages, we will encourage you to change "**Why is this happening to me?**" to "What is this teaching me and how will it improve me?", so that you can receive all the abundance that you deserve and be mentally prepared to grow into your best self.

It is a challenging task to embrace our role as leaders, bosses, executives, entrepreneurs, founders, or owners. It is an extra challenge for us women to reach positions of power and to get treated fairly and equally. However, when faced with these challenges, think about the competitive advantage these setbacks have given you. You have become tougher, wiser, and built more resilience. **You deserve all the abundance that is being poured onto you by the universe** and you need to wear it like a crown, because it is you that got yourself here, and your past self would be proud to see how far you've come.

It is our responsibility to share that there have not only been highs in our story but also lows that we have overcome by pushing forward and finding words of support from other women. We truly hope you enjoy these pages and see them as a guide **to unleash the power that is inside you**, to become the best version of yourself, to overcome all setbacks, and to welcome the success that you deserve.

Sisters Lola & Ana

1
COURAGE

BE BRAVE.

BE BOLD.

BE YOU.

(UNAPOLOGETICALLY.)

Fear can keep us from fulfilling our dreams and living lives full of wonder and greatness. Often, our fear of failure leads us to believe that we are not enough and leave us unable to take advantage of opportunities that may come our way. Courage is about taking the risk to achieve your dreams even though you are afraid of failure. It's not about taking big leaps but about taking those small steps every day that move you toward the life you want. It's okay if you fail during the journey to the life you are hoping to build for yourself. Every failure is a lesson that you can carry with you for the next attempt at achieving your goals.

Sometimes, it can seem as though everyone else has life figured out and you are just straggling behind, but don't let your own thoughts scare you away from an amazing future. Everyone is running their own race and even though it may seem like it's taking you longer, that doesn't mean that what is meant for you is not coming. Don't let negative thoughts make you self-sabotage the greatness that is coming into your life. Your mind is powerful, and it has a way of creating our realities. You cannot live an abundant life while thinking that you are not enough. You call into being what is going to happen.

Don't know where to start? Or does thinking about your goals bring you anxiety? First, bring yourself to a place of calm and take a few deep breaths in and a few deep breaths out. Think of some small steps you can do that can take you closer to your objective. Let's say you want to switch careers, but you have been working in your current industry for a long time or don't know how to go about it. Research how to make the big move; maybe that means getting a new degree or having the right connections. Break your goal down into days, so if you need a new degree, take a few minutes in your day to search schools and requirements for the degree. Take another few minutes the next day to find people in the field that you can contact for advice. Keep going every day until you reach where you want to go.

Bravery is about taking that leap and continuing to keep going even though every step you take feels like a risk. Follow what makes you happy even if it's the scariest thing you have ever done. Be kind to yourself when things don't go as planned and love yourself for your differences—that is what makes you unique. And your uniqueness is what makes you stand out in a crowd. Use that to your advantage to make bold choices and create wonderful things. What skills do you bring to the table that other people don't have? How can you use your skills to make what you want to happen?

Remember that courage is not about being a hero; it's about confronting your biggest challenges and overcoming them a day at a time. We all have courage inside of us, we just have to tap into that part of ourselves. Be brave. Be bold. Be you.

1 COURAGE

When we first started our company, I felt as if we didn't need a team, processes, or any of the key elements that make our company great today. I was afraid of change. What if we failed? But I knew we wanted our business to grow, and I had to be at peace with the fact that in order to grow, we need to accept change, and new results require different techniques. I embraced change by looking at every opportunity for it as a step closer to our goals and progress. I got excited at the possibilities and moved forward with the necessary changes. Today, we're in a better place, we've grown, I find our products in stores and friends' homes all the time, and I sleep knowing that change was the catalyst I needed to go from business school graduate and aspiring artist to Chief Creative Officer of one of America's largest manufacturers of wall décor.

The fear of the unknown can stop us from creating change in our lives, taking new approaches to things, and finding the courage to take risks. **Approach change with curiosity**, **with an eagerness for learning**. How fun is it to have the opportunity to do something new? Think about it like opening a box stored in your attic. An enchanted box, a positive box, and you have no idea what is inside. Perhaps you won't like it, but you should definitely take a peek. Change helps us evolve. If we do nothing, nothing happens. Take the necessary risks to make your dreams happen. **What will you do differently tomorrow?**

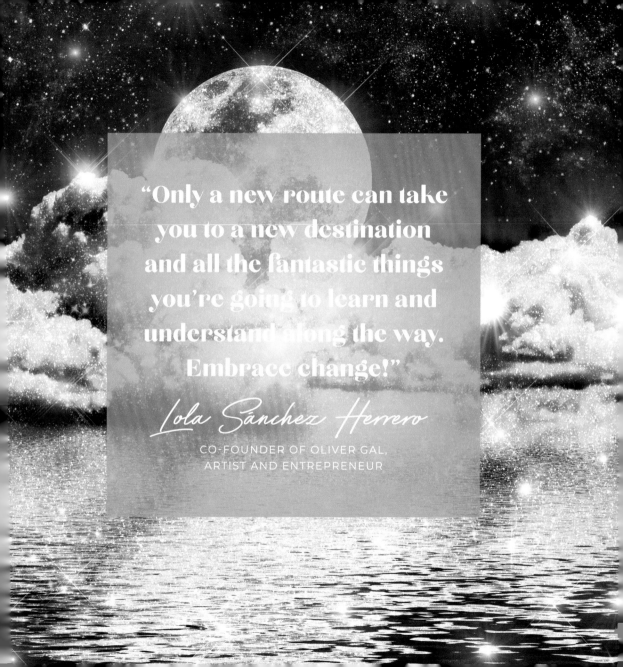

"Only a new route can take you to a new destination and all the fantastic things you're going to learn and understand along the way. Embrace change!"

Lola Sánchez Herrero

CO-FOUNDER OF OLIVER GAL,
ARTIST AND ENTREPRENEUR

1 COURAGE

Cindy Eckert's courageous nature led her to achieve her many successes and she continues to mentor women to encourage them to take on life with bravery every day. By defying conventions that can sometimes be intimidating, she has been able to achieve great things and has become a staple of courage.

If your past self could see how far you've come, **would she have been more courageous?** Would she have risked more? Admire your current state, your situation, and accept what is about to happen, what will come to you—the unknown—with all your heart. Trust the process of growth without questioning every step or fearing those questions that you don't yet have answers for. You won't always have the answers, you weren't born knowing everything you know today, and yet here you are. **Trust your progress**, believe in your growth, and even when you don't have all the answers this will give you the courage to take another step into the future and come closer to success. Maybe that next step is the one that will make all the difference, so it's up to you to build up the courage to take it as if you knew you could not fail. **Walk without fear down the path to your success story**.

What will you do tomorrow that scares you now? What will you do that your future self will thank you for?

"Success doesn't come from having all the answers. Success comes from having courage."

Cindy Eckert

CEO OF THE PINK CEILING AND SPROUT PHARMACEUTICALS

1 COURAGE

Denise Elnajjar had been drawing fashion sketches since she was a child, but her career had taken her elsewhere. She had built a background in international affairs, and it seemed that being an illustrator was out of the picture. It was when she won a New York sketching contest to collaborate with a major eyewear brand that she knew it was a sign to give everything to her dreams. Since then, Denise has worked with clients in the fashion, luxury, and beauty worlds. Her works have been featured by brands like Moschino, L'Oréal, and Giambattista Valli and featured in magazines like *Vogue* Japan and *Cosmopolitan*.

To deviate from the norm or the pack is challenging. Sometimes it means to go where nobody has been before, to step into waters you don't recognize, and it will require bravery. **Don't doubt your strength**. You will find criticism and negativity along the way and most of it might come from your inner self. That eternal fear of failure. Look beyond; what makes you different also makes you truly special, and that is what you should embrace. Don't doubt your talent. Love the difference, **love the unknown**, and have faith in yourself and your dreams. When you boldly look beyond the obstacles, what others are doing, and scary what-ifs, and you focus on your plan and the goal, the path will light up on its own and take you there.

If you are looking for answers, for something to happen, then you must **find courage in your strength**, **your talent, and yourself**. These are the key ingredients to realize your ideas.

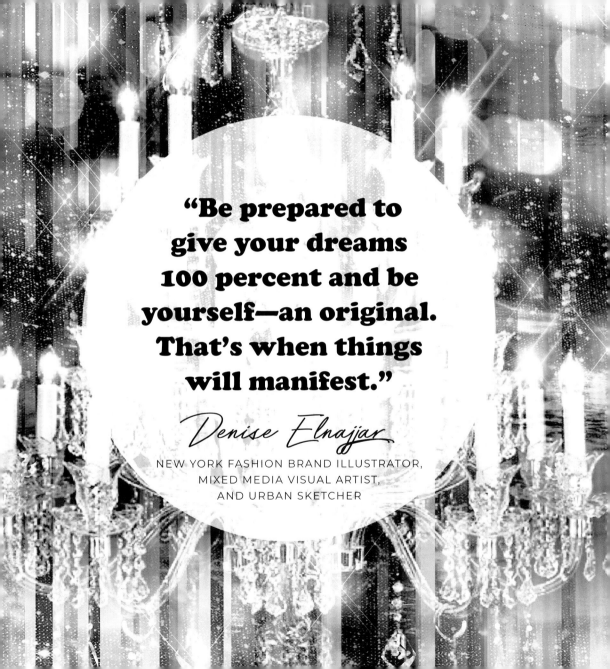

"Be prepared to give your dreams 100 percent and be yourself—an original. That's when things will manifest."

Denise Elnajjar

NEW YORK FASHION BRAND ILLUSTRATOR, MIXED MEDIA VISUAL ARTIST, AND URBAN SKETCHER

1 COURAGE

Born and raised in NYC and a first-generation American, Nathalie Mendez is one of thirteen children. From a young age, she was obsessed with designing spaces and transforming them into an experience for those who entered. During her teenage years, she used her creative outlet to deal with being outcasted by her family for being part of the LGBTQ community. Instead of letting this set her back, she used this as the fuel she needed to ignite the power inside of her and become one of the country's top visual merchandisers and designer of retail spaces.

Once the glitz is gone, the party is over, and reality kicks in, sometimes we might find ourselves alone, out of matches to burn, feeling like there's nothing left. However, there is one thing left—**you**. Only you can harness the power that is inside you, and that in itself is a choice. **Who are you choosing to be, today**? Look at yourself in the mirror; there is what you need, that is who you need, you need to look no further.

You are powerful; what you need is already in you. However, in the end, it will all come down to one decision: **Will you take back your power?**

Will you own that undeniable force inside of you and provide it with a purpose or will you let it lie dormant?

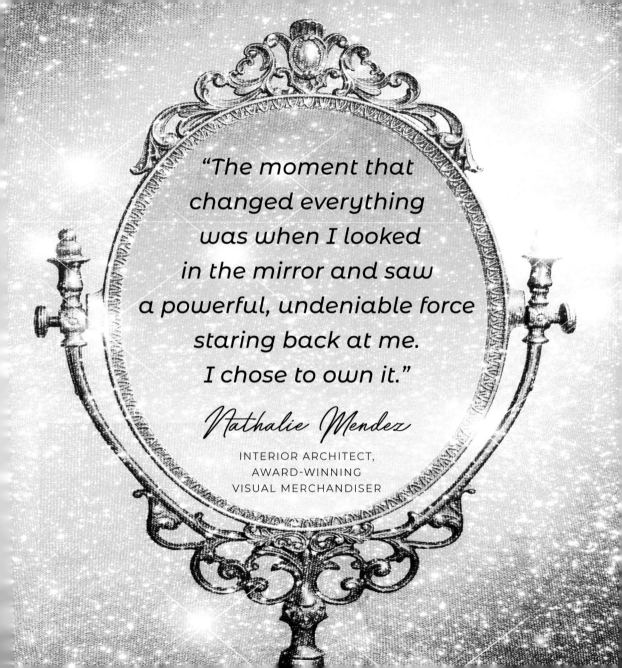

"The moment that changed everything was when I looked in the mirror and saw a powerful, undeniable force staring back at me. I chose to own it."

Nathalie Mendez

INTERIOR ARCHITECT,
AWARD-WINNING
VISUAL MERCHANDISER

As a young woman, Chié Dambara was diagnosed with BRCA—a genetic mutation that increases the chances of developing breast cancer by up to 80 percent. At the age of twenty-four, she had to bravely undergo a double mastectomy with reconstruction to prevent breast cancer. As frightening as it was for her, she was still able to find the power to overcome this scary situation and share her passion for matcha and healthy living with the world. She brought to life her love for green tea and created her own business, Yoko Matcha.

Today her business is thriving, and she also donates a part of their profits to support breast cancer research. In every cup, Chié sees her strength and she shares this with the world.

There are so many stories of brave women who have to battle cancer and face setbacks with all their might. Previvors, survivors, fighters are all getting up one day after another, never losing hope but, more importantly, harnessing all their courage to continue the fight for themselves and others. From their powerful stories we can learn so much and **find the strength inside ourselves to overcome whatever comes our way**.

"It's okay to fall or make mistakes, as long as you get back up every time. Learn from every experience and keep moving forward in strength and bravery."

Chié Dambara

FOUNDER OF YOKO MATCHA,
BRCA SURVIVOR, AND MATCHA VISIONARY

Before being a museum owner, Allison Freidin worked as a lawyer for the male-dominated Miami-Dade Police Department, where she assisted in the preparation and execution of search warrants intended to recover illegal firearms. The risks involved required her to wear a bulletproof vest, and she somehow got used to having that physical protection. Even though she didn't need such extreme protection when she shifted careers to work in the art world, she wished she had some type of armor to protect her from people's judgment and nonconstructive criticism. She knew she couldn't avoid criticism, so she found a way to not let judgments get her down, by creating her own armor of honesty and confidence.

Being honest and embracing who you are with full confidence and unapologetically is fundamental to feeling empowered. Empowered women can reach further goals, go further, and aim higher because they have the confidence, the courage.

Polish your shiny body armor and present yourself to the world as the incredible woman that you are. You have gotten this far, and you haven't shown the world your full-fledged confident and powerful self entirely . . . just yet. Envision your armor before doing something that makes you feel stressed, fearful, or concerned. Envision yourself in your powerful shiny armor taking over that room, conquering that situation. **What does your armor look like?**

"Shiny silver body armor is made from the perfect mix of confidence and honesty."

Allison Freidin

FOUNDER OF
THE MUSEUM OF GRAFFITI

1 COURAGE

There have been many times when Lola Tash—actress, gifted writer, and founder of the meme empire MyTherapistSays—has found herself alone, suffering from anxiety. Instead of recusing herself in her thoughts, she made it a mission to help herself and then others through her initiative MyTherapistHelps, talking openly about mental illness and broadening the conversation by putting her personal story and vulnerability at the forefront.

There may be times when you will feel as if you don't have people around you to support you. There also may be times when you will have to face things alone or lead others who are dependent on you. That is why **the person who ultimately deserves and requires you to give your all to is you**. Read that again, girl.

So many people have achieved so much with what looks to be so little, but they all had something in common, something unquantifiable, that you cannot see with the naked eye—**true**, **genuine self-confidence and determination**. You've heard it so many times: they just didn't know they could fail, so they didn't. Lola Tash turned her anxiety into an ally by believing. She was so focused on the aim, so strong-minded about reaching her goal, and so sure of herself that she not only accomplished what she set out to do, but she also inspired others along the way. Just Like Lola, if you believe in yourself, you, too, can accomplish courageous and amazing things.

"It's been proven, time and again, that belief in yourself is your greatest ally when conquering any great heights. I think it's important that when you look back on your life, on the years in which you were creating all that you've envisioned, you are going to remember that it was all constructed on a foundation of belief, courage, and laughter at all the moments that didn't quite pan out."

Lola Tash

CO-FOUNDER AND CEO OF MYTHERAPISTSAYS, ACTRESS, AND MENTAL HEALTH ADVOCATE

1 COURAGE

Alyce Tran is the perfect woman to talk about planning, thinking, and sometimes overthinking. She had saved over a year's worth of salary before she turned her side hustle into her full-time job, designing and selling customizable accessories and fine stationery. However, she wouldn't have turned her brand into a $23 million powerhouse if it weren't for the courage that her parents instilled in her. Her parents are Vietnamese immigrants who moved to Australia as refugees. They built a real estate empire from nothing and they showed Alyce that courage and a great work ethic will take you further than endless discussions and overthinking or overplanning.

While planning can be a fundamental part of any strategy, sometimes it is necessary to skip that part and **just get going** in order to learn from your mistakes and get used to the iterative process of building a business or completing an objective.

It is so terribly easy to get caught up in talking about possibilities and the chances that something might or might not work, to overthink to the extent that we get paralyzed or that we forget to execute. In plain, we don't get things done!

So set a date, **set a time**, **and just start**, **start doing**, have the work spark more questions, genuine ones, and learn from the process.

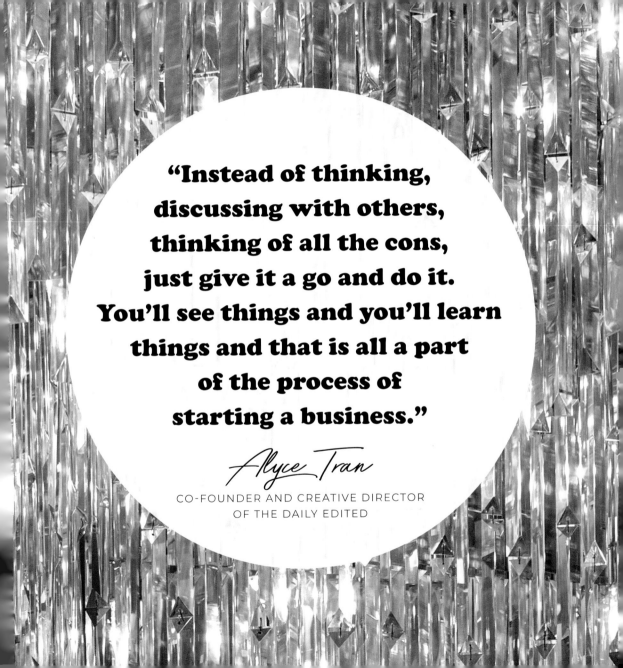

"Instead of thinking, discussing with others, thinking of all the cons, just give it a go and do it. You'll see things and you'll learn things and that is all a part of the process of starting a business."

Alyce Tran

CO-FOUNDER AND CREATIVE DIRECTOR
OF THE DAILY EDITED

1 COURAGE

Dana Randall, the former head of innovation of Tapestry Inc. (Coach, Kate Spade, Stuart Weitzman), is by no means a conventional executive and that is what has landed her numerous awards, speaking engagements all over the world, and the chance to share her unique point of view with others. By embracing her feminine side and all of the idiosyncrasies that make her who she is, she is proving to all of us that being bold enough to be different gives you an innovating edge.

Have you embraced your true self and decided to be above all others' opinions, above established norms, and just been naturally genuine recently? **It requires bravery and willpower to be vulnerable** and allow others to enjoy the true you. Sometimes these moments are tainted by our own mind, making us self-conscious and concerned that we might not meet the expectations. **You are not alone**.

Admit your fears, **your quirkiness**, **your uniqueness**; they will bring you compassion and make you more human and empathetic toward others with similar concerns. Support others who are self-conscious about certain traits in themselves and help them gain the courage necessary to be vulnerable, approachable, and sincere. **Prove to yourself**, through courage, that these traits you proudly carry are completely unrelated to your business skills. This will open many doors to ways that will allow you to achieve whatever you set your mind to.

"Every morning I wake up with a personal mission to be brave enough to truly be myself. Whether it's dyeing my hair pink or covering my walls in glitter, I do my best to tackle each day being unapologetically myself. But don't mistake my love for pretty pink sparkly things as a lack of hard-hitting business chops."

Dana Randall

VENTURE PARTNER AT ALLEY VENTURES,
INNOVATOR, AND CREATOR

1 COURAGE

Frankie Cihi is an internationally recognized, Japanese-American painter of surreal landscapes and colorful patterns. Her paintings are displayed everywhere from small galleries to Google offices to Starbucks's themed shops. All of her artwork displays the fearlessness and bravery of her passion and process in creating them.

When she was commissioned to do a hand painting of a half-mile-long mural spanning a parking garage, she said yes, even though she had never done it before. But she had to know whether she could, right? So, she made the bold decision to do it, and today, her parking garage mural has made the Travel Channel's list of "10 Amazing Urban Transformations."

You might procrastinate and overthink whether to do something, using the excuse of lack of inspiration or negative thoughts about your ability to do it or not to. Reframe this overthinking; tame your thoughts by starting. Don't let your mind wander on negative thoughts: get to it, **make the bold move**, take the chance. Inspiration will come knocking, and it will find you working, creating, ready to absorb its power, and you will get the results you're looking for.

"AIN'T NOTHING TO IT BUT TO DO IT!"

Frankie Cihi
aka Furpuff

VISUAL ARTIST, TV PERSONALITY,
AND MURALIST

2

LEADERSHIP

KEEP HUSTLIN', GIRL.

(YOU'RE UNSTOPPABLE.)

What makes someone a leader? When most people think about leadership, they think of someone who has a lot of money or owns a multimillion-dollar business, and while that is great, leadership is about much more than that. Yes, leadership is about achieving astonishing things, but what makes someone a great leader is their ability to guide others to succeed too. Being a leader is about being the kind of person that everyone aspires to be like or someone that can inspire another person to do something amazing. A leader is a person who leads people to believe the impossible can become possible.

Think of all the amazing people in your life and who and what about them inspires you to do things you never thought you could. What can you take from them? You can do great things and accomplish what you set your mind to. Own your power and use it to be the kind of leader that sets the world ablaze. Inspire younger generations to look up to you and want to do better for themselves and their community. Being able to give back to your community is also another way to lead those around you to greatness. It gives you the opportunity to interact with and meet different people from varying backgrounds while also acknowledging the needs of your community. Noticing what needs to be improved leads to powerful change, and can lead you to become an ambassador to those in need. It only takes one person to stand up. One person to change a reality. One person to make a difference.

Trust in yourself and in your talents. Be the leader you want to be through action, understanding, compassion, and accountability. You are more powerful than you imagine. You have all the power you need inside of you already. All you have to do is to tap into it and use it. Don't be afraid of making mistakes. We are only human, and no human is perfect. Use your mistakes to create a better future.

Owning who you are and using your inner power is what makes the most incredible opportunities manifest themselves. Keep being resilient and show your strength. Show the world how amazing you are and the kinds of things you can accomplish. It is not about saving the world or doing that big thing; it's about those small changes and steps you take to make amazing things happen. Be confident in yourself and your beliefs. Use your confidence to keep you going. When you are confident, you are clear on your intentions and your goals. It is what makes us leaders—the ability to lead with clarity, focus, and intention.

Leadership is not about holding a specific title. It's about being able to empower yourself and others to be the best they can be. It's about having the courage to be different and aspiring others to be different too. Own the inner you and be the leader you are meant to be.

2 LEADERSHIP

Zeina El-Dana is a seasoned entrepreneur who fosters collaboration and a sense of ownership and belonging. In her company, there's no judgment, no idea too small, no hierarchal boundaries—everyone has the opportunity to contribute, at whatever level. This helps her business move forward fast while being extremely flexible. Her team comes to work feeling happy and ready to take on anything. Zeina leads with their well-being in mind, allowing them to own their decision and enabling her team to own it.

"Owning it" means that **everything starts and ends with you**—your decisions, your life, your situation. You are one thought, one decision away from change, from improvement. And the same applies to failures and mistakes. Every individual is responsible for their mistakes, and while we will help each other out in times of distress or difficult situations, we will only do so if the responsible person owns their mistake and is willing to learn from it and help themselves.

This is applicable to every aspect of life; it is better to teach somebody how to do something than to do it for them. **Support others to empower themselves** with the knowledge that you have acquired and have them own their future and past. This builds character and independence, two very important qualities that don't come preinstalled in us.

Change your mentality to the "own it" mentality and, suddenly, everything is up to you! That makes possibilities unlimited.

"Being a business owner is really about 'owning' everything you do—developing your team, serving your clients, growing your business. Only then you'll find the right people to join you."

Zeina El-Dana

CEO OF Z7 COMMUNICATIONS
AND DUBAI STYLE ICON

2 LEADERSHIP

Emily Roberts is always on the lookout for bold trends, and she uses her platform to inspire women to take risks, make moves, and not be afraid to be unique—to lead in their field and not follow the pack. Many times, we try to focus on improving the common traits that we share with our competitors to make ourselves better, instead of highlighting our differences and what truly makes our company stand out.

Think about what makes you special—the thing or things that make you unique. **You are the queen** of that market because nobody else is you. Only you can provide this particular product or service. If you approach your business, or even life, like this, you will become priceless.

There are times when we think we must follow everyone else's steps to get to a certain point, an intention or a goal, and that is simply not true. So, when you feel like you don't fit in, that is actually great news! Find your talent, your skill, practice it, improve it, make it into something so rare that you find customers or followers just because of it.

What makes you or your company different? Got it? Great, now go and spread that sparkle!

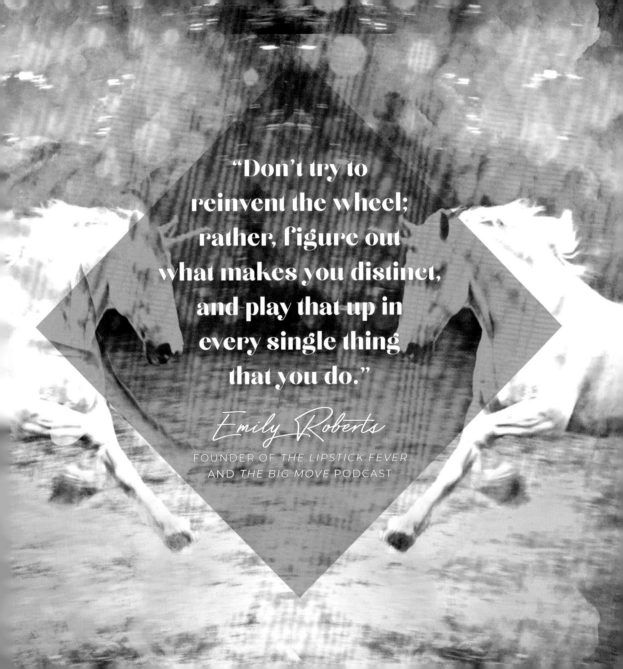

"Don't try to reinvent the wheel; rather, figure out what makes you distinct, and play that up in every single thing that you do."

Emily Roberts

FOUNDER OF *THE LIPSTICK FEVER* AND *THE BIG MOVE* PODCAST

2 LEADERSHIP

Linda Comp-Noto is no stranger to the gender gap. As an executive woman, she is part of the TP Women board, an initiative that stands behind diversity, inclusion, and gender balance, supporting equal opportunity and participation.

There is no progress toward growth when we don't push for it; the world is filled with inequality and it is our duty to reduce the gap. As women, one of the injustices we have to fight is gender inequality. When we help and support each other, we are positively impacting one another with the confidence to stand up and progress to a brighter future. Initiatives such as TP Women, pave the way for a better future.

Every instance of disrespect or unfairness should inspire us to continue to make a better world for the next girls, the future women, because after all, this is the legacy they will inherit and what will make our stories live on forever.

Teach younger women what you would have loved to know when you were their age; be that leader and that helping hand to prepare the next generation. It is sometimes one word, one action, one situation that inspires somebody's future. **Be a leader, and encourage future leaders**.

"True success in business happens when all people can choose to experience successful career growth regardless of gender, race, or religion. It is up to us as leaders to create the platform to do so."

Linda Comp-Noto

DIVISION PRESIDENT AT TELEPERFORMANCE
AND TP WOMEN BOARD MEMBER

2 LEADERSHIP

Isabel Harris worked on Wall Street for years and was used to being the only woman in the room. She was frequently left out of career opportunities because she was a Hispanic woman with an accent. She used this to drive her to continue onward, pursuing her career and making a wonderful life for herself. Now, Isabel spends most of her time being a mom and working as a partner for her firm, PH Consulting, where she takes a creative leadership role—her real passion. She never lets anyone's negative perception of her change her objectives.

As much as the world has made progress in equality for women in the workplace during the past hundred years, we still have so much work to do to be part of the change. Discrimination is a constant reality we have to face. While you won't always be everyone's favorite, and while you might encounter people who try to dim your light, let that judgment from others **fuel your desire to change the world and shatter stereotypes**. Prove them wrong, kill them with kindness, and make a difference that will ripple in others' lives.

Set up future generations for success. You do not have to adapt to the negative energy being projected onto you; you can beam positive energy and be an inspiration to everyone you encounter. You can lead by example. **Remember**, **if you can dream it, you can achieve it**.

"NEVER LET ANYONE ELSE'S NARROW VIEWS DIM YOUR GOALS. IF YOU CAN DREAM IT, YOU CAN ACHIEVE IT."

Isabel Harris

MOM, PARTNER AT PH CONSULTING, AND FORMER VICE PRESIDENT OF MARKETING AT OXYGEN BIOTHERAPEUTICS

2 LEADERSHIP

Alexx Kann was born in Florida and raised in France by German parents. From a young age, she discovered many different cultures, met intriguing people, and learned to speak foreign languages. After living in a variety of cities, she settled in Miami Beach, which turned out to be full of opportunities. But ultimately this glamorous and sometimes superficial life did not satisfy her, so she decided to lead her life in a different direction and leave the comfort and amenities of Miami behind. After organizing the perfect departure, she set sail to Asia without a particular destination in mind. While on her travels, she visited Cambodia and fell in love with the small island of Koh Rong Samloem.

Cambodia was a dream come true—despite its turbulent past, it is now a haven of peace and tranquility paired with boundless beauty and friendly people. Opportunity knocked and Alexx bought a small guest house-type hotel directly on the beach. It took stamina and perseverance for her to polish the property into a shining jewel. Today, her business is thriving, and she combines work with her passion to invest in her village's infrastructure and growth by raising funds to help local families.

When you are ready to change after a long and maybe unsatisfying journey, just do it. **You are the leading character of your story**. The most amazing and marvelous creations, innovations, and progress have come from those who continued after all others gave up. Stand up, shake the dust off, and tell yourself "**Just one more time**," because it is that one, the unexpected one, the one that will change everything, that ultimate attempt before reaching success, the one that will make you a doer, a changer, a leader.

"Life is an adventure. You are the main character, leading your story, so make your dreams come true and live your 1001 lives."

Alexx Kann

HOTEL OWNER AT MY WAY CAMBODIA
AND WORLD EXPLORER

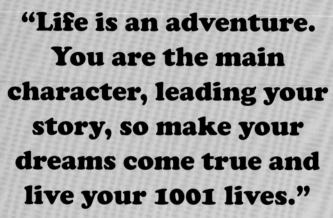

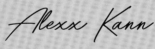

Lin Jerome obtained a law degree from Boyd School of Law and turned down six-figure job offers to pursue what she knew was her future—opening a marketing agency. Even though she had an opportunity to make money to pay off her student loan debt, she still chose her passion. Every single time she ran into an issue, she knew she had chosen this harder path to success. She treated failure as an opportunity instead of another reason to go back to the legal sector. Today, Lin sits on the Founding Board of the Women's Hospitality Initiative and has become one of Las Vegas's top female entrepreneurs, owning not only a marketing agency but also a few hospitality ventures.

It is only when you can overcome difficulties that you are able to set a precedent for yourself and others that it can be done. **Failure is a privilege** because it offers us lessons that help us succeed. It is a sign that you are on the right path, on the path of trying, of doing, of learning.

Failure is a "learning opportunity" or "growth challenge" because you are on your way and, soon, you will prove your naysayers wrong and show them that **from many failures and perseverance comes greatness**. Congratulations! You've been blessed with failure: how are you going to learn from this and how much closer are you now to figuring out how to make it a success?

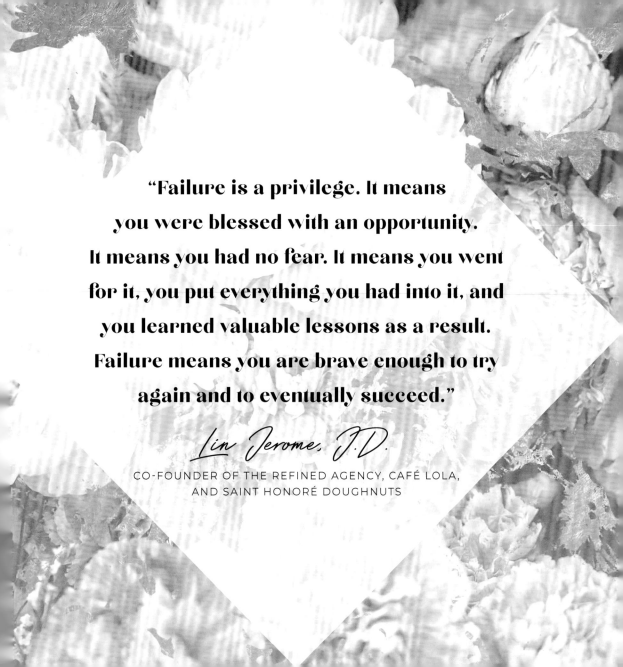

"Failure is a privilege. It means
you were blessed with an opportunity.
It means you had no fear. It means you went
for it, you put everything you had into it, and
you learned valuable lessons as a result.
Failure means you are brave enough to try
again and to eventually succeed."

Lin Jerome, J.D.

CO-FOUNDER OF THE REFINED AGENCY, CAFÉ LOLA,
AND SAINT HONORÉ DOUGHNUTS

2 LEADERSHIP

Itziar Fuentes bet it all in 2014 to start an urban fashion brand in her hometown of Marbella, Spain. At that time, she knew she had one shot, so she put in all her savings and gave it all she had. All her hard work has paid off and she just opened her first store in Saudi Arabia. It wasn't an overnight success, and it may have taken her many tries, failures, and lessons learned to get there, but her patience, skills, and fierce determination assured her well-deserved triumphs.

Social media has made success look ubiquitous; it looks like everyone is living the perfect dream. You can feel inspired, and at the same time demotivated, because it may seem like you're the odd one out. As if you're not working hard enough or like success is never going to happen for you. But the truth is, **success is a recipe that takes a long time to cook**, that requires a lot of ingredients, and all to ultimately look like it was put together overnight by lady luck. We are all walking our own paths, and it's not fair to yourself to compare your journey to someone else's.

If you are going through a lot of work, difficulties, and pains and you're wondering whether it's worth it . . . the answer is yes. No breakthrough ever came on the first try. So, if you're unsure whether the path you took is the right one because it's so hard, **keep on going**, **keep on pushing**, **keep on learning**; you're better than who you were yesterday. You're on your way. Give yourself a round of applause and a good night's sleep. You deserve it. Just don't forget that tomorrow will be **rise and grind time**.

"Success in anything requires time, heartache, pain, patience, skills, and a ton of lessons learned along the way. It's not easy. It's not quick, it's not always fun, and it's not for everyone. Don't be so hard on yourself; just get it together and go for it."

Itziar Fuentes

CO-FOUNDER AND CEO OF HOMIES MARBELLA AND BRANDING MAVERICK

2 LEADERSHIP

Marianna Bracco moved to the US from her native Brazil and has the firm belief that being a woman is the secret ingredient to multitasking your way to success. However, having worked for some of the largest design brands in the country and lived in three different US cities, she realized the need to have a **circle of trust**, a group of women that she could rely on and with whom she could discuss the challenges she was facing.

She co-founded her nonprofit organization, A Seat At The Table, where great women thinkers discuss, offer advice, provide a sounding board, and support each other. It is through her support circle and her strong determination to follow her gut that she shapes her reality toward almost guaranteed success.

Create your own support circle. By doing this, you are cementing positive relationships with other aspirational people that will help you look at different perspectives, give you trustworthy advice, and give you some motivation in times of doubt. **Set new and powerful goals in your mind**, embrace them, channel your actions through them, and soon your whole universe will rearrange itself to fit your new reality. **Trust your intuition**, your supporters, and follow the path to your dreams. You are ready: take the first step and watch the universe conspire toward your success!

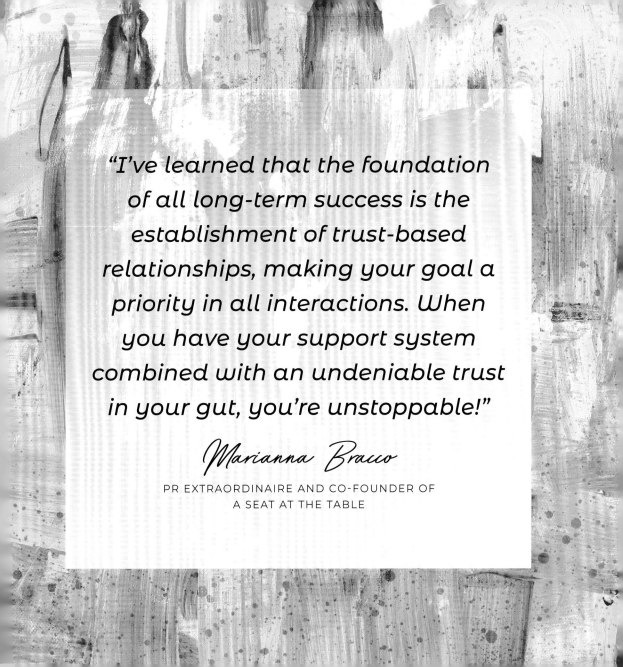

"I've learned that the foundation of all long-term success is the establishment of trust-based relationships, making your goal a priority in all interactions. When you have your support system combined with an undeniable trust in your gut, you're unstoppable!"

Marianna Bracco

PR EXTRAORDINAIRE AND CO-FOUNDER OF
A SEAT AT THE TABLE

2 LEADERSHIP

Michelle Abbs decided to be an educator early in life. She grew up in Michigan and saw inequality from her own backyard, looking at the fence that divided a wealthy suburban area from a greater urban one. Since then, her vision has been to be a balanced leader who leads through education and by example in order to reduce the inequality she saw growing up.

As the former director of Babson College's Accelerator Program, she has had the chance to create countless women leaders, instilling in them the importance to execute as well as lead. Currently, she is leading a project to build a tech hub in downtown Miami, led by visionary entrepreneur Moishe Mana. She hopes the vision of the project will inspire more leaders.

Focus on being balanced, on offering as much advice, counsel, and leadership as displaying the **true power of doing and moving the needle forward as an individual**. This will inspire others to follow suit. Work theories and business advice are just opinions and thoughts, but **true effort lies in execution**, proving that operating as part of the team alongside leading it and empowering its individuals will help you become the leader you seek to be, the one that will make it happen.

"The best leaders are masters of balance, specifically of opposing ideas. They are equally skilled at listening and giving direction. They are equally skilled at empowering a team and operating as an individual. The best leaders are skilled on both sides of any equation."

Michelle Abbs

DIRECTOR OF MANA TECH MIAMI

2 LEADERSHIP

There is leadership potential in all of us, but being a leader is the hardest of jobs and the heaviest of responsibilities. It requires walking the fine line of balance between opposites: soft and hard, optimistic and pragmatic. Everyone can grow to be a leader, to inspire others and make a difference, to **change one speck of history**. To be a leader, you have to be thoughtful of others, treat people with respect, and inspire love and dedication to the work you do. It also requires you to hold the group's purpose above your own, to sometimes be able to make tough calls for the greater good of the group, and overall to leave your own ego outside the door and recognize when you are wrong.

Leading a team of creatives at Oliver Gal and seeing how they lead their own direct reports has taught me that **there is no one-size-fits-all leadership mode**, but the key is to focus on what the person you're leading needs at that moment in relation to the problem or situation they're facing.

In my experience, if you can be vulnerable when you must and strong when you need to, then be a leader. **Take charge**. **Inspire**. Because there is no greater good than inspiring others to do better, to do great things. That is what you can do. What a leader does.

"Leadership means to inspire while you grind, to listen while you build the plan, to empower others while you teach the way, to care while you execute the plan, turning your vision into life."

Lola Sánchez Herrero

CO-FOUNDER OF OLIVER GAL, ARTIST,
AND ENTREPRENEUR

3
PURPOSE

LIVING

THE

DREAM.

(W I T H   L O V E   &   P U R P O S E .)

Purpose is the why of our existence and our reason for being here on this Earth. It is one of life's existential questions. While some of us may have already found our purpose, a lot of us are still searching for our why. Living a life full of purpose helps us feel fulfilled and brings joy to our every day. A life without purpose can make us feel defeated, depressed, and empty.

Figuring out your why will help you live a life full of passion. It can be intimidating to think that you may never find what you are here to do. But we all have a purpose and talents to share with the world. Some of us can find purpose from our jobs or our careers, but it is not necessarily defined by what you do for a living, although loving what you do is a big part of living a fulfilled life. Others may find their purpose from a cause or a mission that they feel strongly connected to.

Your soul will call to you strongly once you find something that leads you to the direction of your why. Every step you take closer to your purpose will ignite the fire inside of you. Once you find a hint of your purpose, keep taking steps towards it.

If you are unhappy and feel empty where you are right now, search for things that make you feel joy. It is through these things that you will able to find your gifts. For example, if you are not satisfied with the industry that you are in, research other industries that catch your interest. It may feel like it's impossible to change careers or follow the path you were meant to follow, but don't let your doubts get in the way of what you are meant to do in life. Sometimes it is just a matter stopping yourself from self-sabotaging to go after what you really want.

Take the necessary risks to accomplish what you want out of life. Only then can you discover the thing that makes you feel excited about waking up the next day. You will know when you find it because time won't matter when you are doing what brings you happiness.

Ask yourself: "What drives me?" and think of the things that people are continually coming to you for. What talents and skills do you offer? When you have a clear answer to these questions, you will be able to move closer to your purpose and find meaning in your life.

The road to your why won't always be an easy one. You will feel lost at times, but as long as you are taking meaningful steps toward your purpose, you will find it, or it will find its way to you. The universe has a way of bringing us what we need in due time. Keep exploring, keep moving forward, and you will see rewarding results.

We are all meant to live fulfilling lives full of joy, abundance, and peace. When we find what we are looking for, we are better for it, we radiate it out into the world, and we see all the amazing possibilities life has to give us. You are worthy of your purpose.

3 PURPOSE

When I started one of my first companies, AllPopArt.com, we were profitable. My husband and I employed over ten people and had provided beautiful personalized artwork to thousands of customers. However, I had no path to citizenship and my work visa was about to expire, which would hinder me from continuing to lead the company and pursue my dreams as an artist. The entrepreneur life, such a roller coaster—my company takes off and I'm soon going to be asked to pack up and leave. I kept asking myself how I was going to find the strength to continue when my situation depended on something I didn't understand.

When going through times like these, where it seems like the solution is out of reach, **look at the problem from a different point of view**, discuss it with as many people as possible, and make sure you are not creating any personal constraints or roadblocks when looking for a solution. By doing this, I found out through a friend about the extraordinary ability visa—a visa that I qualified for and that could benefit from all the publications that had featured my company.

I applied and composed my case as if my life depended on it (in a way, to me, it did!) and processed it through Immigration. Even though it was not an easy process, my visa was accepted. Today, I am not only a proud citizen of the United States but also a serial entrepreneur. I was able to further my dreams as a businessowner and pursue my passion for art. **I found my purpose:** to build a team with meaningful jobs and a company that manufactures products that people love.

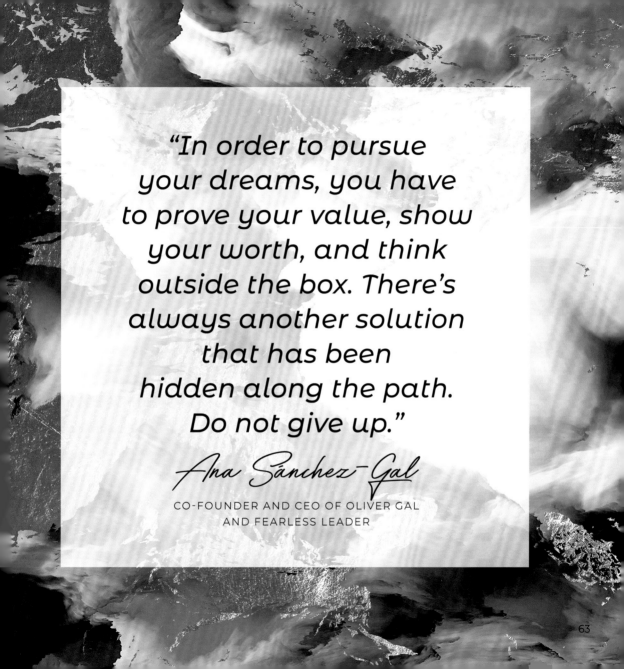

"In order to pursue your dreams, you have to prove your value, show your worth, and think outside the box. There's always another solution that has been hidden along the path. Do not give up."

Ana Sánchez-Gal

CO-FOUNDER AND CEO OF OLIVER GAL
AND FEARLESS LEADER

3 PURPOSE

Alena Capra is an interior designer celebrity, an award-winning industry member, and a TV host and show participant, but she has never let any of these achievements get in the way of giving any of her projects her very best. Whether it's for a client or for a charitable cause, her work exudes passion and genuine care. She is a firm advocate that doing her best and making it her purpose to absolutely wow her clients has in turn given her amazing opportunities that she never expected.

The difference between being good and being absolutely wonderful at something lies in **having the bravery** to exploit that talent and utilize it for the greater good, for something beyond your own benefit. Before taking on your day, **remind yourself of the reason for doing this**, the ultimate beneficiary, and all the other people whose lives you're improving because of your actions, and inevitably success will follow.

Throughout history, we have called it karma, the law of attraction, or positivity, among other things, but it all refers to **giving out what we expect to receive**. Exuding love and sharing joy wherever you go will make the universe react positively and return to you the same, in abundance, and through it you will find your purpose.

"The one thing that matters the most is the relationships you build with people along your journey. The power of kindness toward others is something that will often come back to you in great ways, and usually when you least expect it. It may present itself in the form of opportunities, business, referrals, or possibly even that big break!"

Alena Capra

INTERIOR DESIGNER, TV HOST, AND
OWNER OF ALENA CAPRA DESIGNS

3 PURPOSE

Nicole Jarecz studied at the College for Creative Studies in Detroit and learned about fashion illustration through her art history class. She was captivated by it, but she soon found that there was no fashion illustration program at her school in 2008. She truly believed this was her purpose: she understood her inspiration came from the feeling of observing fashion designs, models, their gestures and movement, and— she wanted to pursue this and learn more about it. Eventually, she found a mentor who helped her do an independent study and she was able, against all odds, to follow her dream and become a fashion illustrator. Today her art can be frequently found in the Saks and Neiman Marcus catalogs and throughout the pages of fashion magazines like *Marie Claire* and *Glamour*.

While the unknown might be discouraging at times, this is a good reminder to **keep the unknown as a source of motivation** to keep on learning and to stay humble, because we still have a long way to go and there is a lot we just don't know! To illustrate this concept, which would you find more exciting: a game whose score has already been decided or a match that keeps you on your toes until the last second?

Find the fire in the unpredictable, **look for the hunger to continue pursuing your dreams and the patience to trust the journey** as you follow your purpose, and your goals will be attained and give meaning to your life.

"It's okay to be lost, and it's okay to take your time, as long as you never give up trying to find your passion and direction in life."

Angela Choi

HONG KONG STYLE ICON AND CEO
OF ATOM CREATIVE

3 PURPOSE

Fatinah Hayat was always interested in fashion and climbed the corporate ladder to work at a prominent jeans manufacturer. While she had reached a level of what many would call success, she wasn't fulfilled and her lifestyle was starting to take a toll on her health, leaving her with a void and a feeling of loneliness. A family trip to Cape Town, a city where water is notoriously scarce, led her to realize she was working for a denim brand that used several gallons of water to produce one pair of jeans, while people in the world were struggling to gain access to clean, drinkable water. As soon as she was back in London, she quit her job and started thinking about how to start her own, ethical fashion company.

It was mindless scrolling that led her to a retreat in Bali, where she did a workshop on Ikigai—a Japanese method on finding your purpose in life. Her company, The Hayat, was born out of her realization of her love for fashion but also her need to venture on an environmentally friendly concept that worked directly with the manufacturers and allowed her to learn about them and their lives and share these lessons with the world. The Hayat is a brand that works directly with artisans, making sure they are paid fairly and that the profits from the sale of their products continue to give back to the community. **Fatinah found her true passion and it showed her that the world needs more kindness and community**. Finding your why can help you find meaning, clarity, and fulfillment in life. **Look for your why in doing the things you enjoy** and make a difference.

"A POWERFUL WHY WILL HELP YOU OVERCOME ANYTHING."

Fatinah Hayat

FOUNDER OF THE HAYAT, IN
LONDON, AND ETHICAL
FASHION ADVOCATE

3 PURPOSE

Elle Blinova's talent has continuously allowed her to explore many different industries throughout her career, from hospitality, to art, and even to real estate. It wasn't until she looked inside of herself and really analyzed the things that made her heart jump that she realized her true purpose was in having her own dress designing brand. We are in a continuous search for that which makes us unique, the one attribute that makes us different or special. Most of us, when we look for this trait, we look at what others see. We take an external position toward finding that hidden gem inside of us.

We all have something completely unique to bring to the table, to share with others, and to cultivate and grow. The key lies in doing some introspective work. What do you like? **What truly brings you alive, and makes you feel energized even if others consider it a tedious task?** That is your power, that is what you can share with the world and use to help contribute to a happier future for your community. Stop looking for your purpose in other people, in external explanations, and look deep to find "**what sets your soul on fire**," the true source of energy you need to power your future and provide meaning in your life.

You are unique by birth, special in every way, and nobody has the talent that you've been given. Therefore, what are you waiting for? **Discover your talent**, look deep inside your soul to find it, and then work on it to master it. When you take what makes you unique and apply it to a higher purpose, **you become unstoppable**.

"There's only one you in this universe. Let that sink in. Get to know yourself. Find what sets your soul on fire. Tune in to your innate energy source and feel your intended future in the present moment. Everything is possible."

Elle Blinova

MARKETING DIRECTOR AT CRESCENT HEIGHTS

3 PURPOSE

Tiffany Pratt is a colorful designer of wonderful spaces and things, and the personification of how change can be beautiful. She uses her creative talent to demonstrate that there is beauty in chaos, love in change, and purpose in continued evolution. Through her designs and her book, *This Can Be Beautiful*, she proves that change can be the way to revive lost causes or situations that make us feel trapped. **There is nothing worse than being somewhere where you have no purpose**. You'll feel stuck, suffocated, down, and without motivation.

Without change, you get comfortable with where you are and take a back seat to living a life full of purpose. You are letting your circumstances and whatever or whoever is around you take the reins of your life and decide for you. While you are waiting in the sidelines, others are being blessed with opportunities. Don't wonder about their luck. It's not luck.

If you want things to happen, **you need to let the universe know that you are ready**, that you want what's out there for you, and the way to express this is to make moves, to materialize your goals and to take the first step toward progress. Only then will you start receiving and experiencing the true meaning of your purpose in life and the color it will bring to your days.

"You cannot just expect things to happen in your life. You need to happen in your life, it's all just a colorful dream anyway. You have nothing to lose. Throw ideas around. Do the damn thing. See what happens. Love might spill out."

Tiffany Pratt

DESIGNER, ARTIST, TV PERSONALITY, SPEAKER, MAKER, AND RAINBOW FAIRY

3 PURPOSE

Jelizaveta Kozlova has established a career in the fashion and luxury brand industry. She holds several degrees, including a Media and Marketing degree from the University of Cambridge and a Luxury and Fashion Brand Management degree from Istituto Marangoni. There once came a time when she had to make a decision about her career when she was offered the opportunity to change industries. But she followed her intuition and decided to stay within her career path to keep pursuing what she loves. This led to her founding EK Laboratory, a boutique consulting agency with end-to-end digital production, marketing communications, and social solutions for fashion and luxury brands.

Whenever you come to a crossroads or a key decision point, knowing who you are and what you are passionate about deep inside at your core will help you make the decision that will make you happier in the long run. Our gut speaks to us by transmitting feelings—excitement, trust, or dislike. You are not being judgmental or too careful if you feel that something is not for you—even if you cannot explain why. **Trust your inner feelings**, they know something that you haven't realized yet.

Use your intuition to gain insight into any decision you make. Ask yourself whether that decision makes you feel good, energized, joyful. Do you really want this? If you had an amazing alternative (let's say a winning lottery ticket) would you still do it? If the answer is no, then dig into how it doesn't align with your core values and who you are at the root. **Remember, nobody knows you as well as you know yourself**.

"Trust your inner feelings when it comes to long-term commitments— choose who you are and what you are passionate about at the base. That will keep your spark alive."

Jelizaveta Kozlova

FOUNDER AND MARKETING DIRECTOR
OF EK LABORATORY

3 PURPOSE

Beth Shaw helped make yoga a mainstream practice in the fitness industry over twenty years ago. Many books, companies, and philanthropic ventures later, she continues to follow her purpose of healing the world and changing lives for the better. Even while being at the forefront of the wellness industry, she faces difficulties every day. Recently, she found herself trapped in a terrible contract with a franchise company that was licensing her name, and she came close to losing everything she had built. Despite all odds being against her, she signed up for a program at Harvard and when she returned, she knew she had to work on getting out of that fifteen-year contract. She set an intention to resolve this issue, took the action, and succeeded in taking her brand back.

You are what you express and manifest, **what you think**, **and wish**, **or pray for**. Sometimes things take time, and you might be on the verge of giving up, but hold on; you must trust the process and continue manifesting those good vibes and positive thoughts. Just as Beth did with intention, will, and action.

It is coming to you, it will, and when the time comes, everything will make sense. The universe develops like a good movie, the plot twist is yet to appear. You will be so happy you continued to exercise a positive attitude and a grateful mentality. **Manifest what you want to receive and be patient: it's on its way**.

"THE UNIVERSE DOES DELIVER—JUST SET THE INTENTION AND WAIT . . . AS IT'S RARELY ON OUR TIME . . . IT'S UNIVERSAL TIME!"

Beth Shaw

FOUNDER OF YOGAFIT, WELLNESS ENTREPRENEUR, EDUCATOR, AND AUTHOR

3 PURPOSE

Jen Stoeckert founded Minimal Beauty in 2015 with the goal of enlightening others about pure and simple beauty care and routines. She is a firm believer in simplification, embracing what is and what isn't working from it. Her brand and philosophy represent this concept of owning your story, knowing that what is coming is what you need and embracing it. She knew from the beginning that it was her fate to encourage others through her brand and she pursued her dream, becoming the holistic beauty expert she is today.

Overthinking and letting anxiety take over your thoughts blurs your vision and goals with unlikely scenarios. It is the worst enemy of progress and growth. **Own your story, focus on your why**, don't overthink what you cannot control, and accept where you are as a starting point. **Accept your situation and let it fuel your future**. Understand that your reason for starting something will keep coming back through your journey. Let it motivate you to continue no matter what comes. Times will be tough and remembering this why constantly and making it the center of your thoughts will help you clarify, your life's purpose, and ultimately what your aspirations are.

Every time you feel negative, with unproductive thoughts clouding your judgment, **go back to your why**, to how you got to where you are today, and refocus your thoughts. Continue working toward your purpose— you should be proud of how far you've gotten and excited about where you're going. You have so much to offer. **Your why will guide the journey and light the way**.

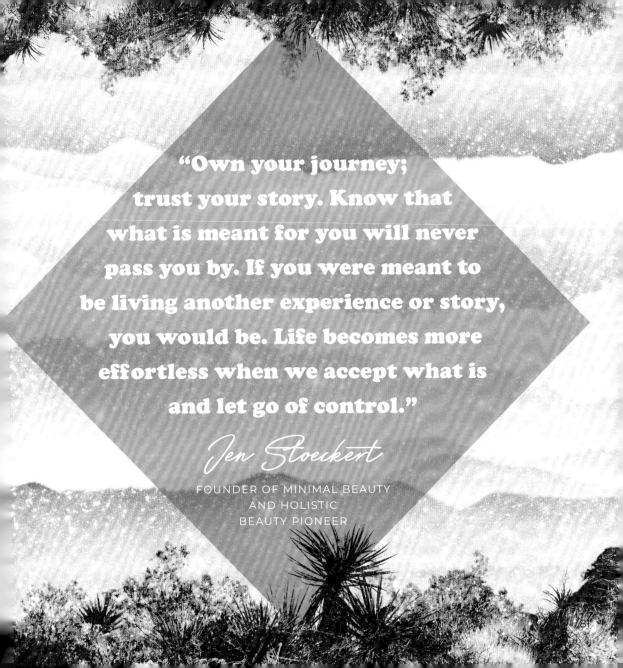

"Own your journey; trust your story. Know that what is meant for you will never pass you by. If you were meant to be living another experience or story, you would be. Life becomes more effortless when we accept what is and let go of control."

Jen Stoeckert

FOUNDER OF MINIMAL BEAUTY
AND HOLISTIC
BEAUTY PIONEER

4
SELF-CARE

WORK HARD. RELAX HARDER.

(LOVE YOURSELF FIRST.)

It's easy to get caught up in the hustle and bustle of today's world. We are constantly on the go, fulfilling some obligation in our schedule. It can feel like we have no time for ourselves or just rest. Self-care is an important part of living a healthy and joyous life. When we find time to rest, our brains function better, we are calmer, and we are less likely to experience stress.

It's crucial that we find time to put ourselves first and be able to give ourselves and our bodies some love. Be kind to your body, be kind to you. The more you offer yourself grace, the more abundance you will find in your life. Self-care can be as simple as taking your lunch break, going outside to get some fresh air, going to bed a few minutes earlier, or taking a break from social media.

Prioritize rest and let go of the need to be busy all the time. You will have time to complete everything you need to without exhausting yourself. Take mini breaks whenever you can to clear your mind. Be more mindful of your body's capacity. Just because you are doing a million things at once doesn't mean that you are being productive. Focus on doing one thing at a time. Choose the most important things to knock off your schedule and hold everything else for another time. Do a digital detox or only check your phone for important messages and emails; this way you don't have any distractions and you're more productive throughout the day.

If you have trouble sleeping, meditate for a few minutes before bed. Just a few minutes of meditation can transform your energy and help you feel relaxed. When you feel like there's too much going on, just take a breath, and meditate to focus your thinking. Keep a journal and take some time to write in it before you take a nap or fall asleep. Writing down your feelings, worries, and thoughts can help you unwind and quiet your mind, so you have a restful night of sleep.

Don't feel bad about carving out time for yourself. Think of the person you love most in the world. What would you do to show that person you care? Do the same thing for yourself. You are deserving of self-love, consideration, rest, and joy. You can't be happy if you are burned out. Don't compromise your well-being to make other people happy. Don't hesitate to let people know when you are in need of "me" time. You are deserving of all the self-love and care.

You are who you put out there. You can't live a life full of abundance if your body and mind are lacking what they need. Give space for self-care in your daily routine and give yourself time to rejuvenate. Once you start prioritizing self-care, you will notice a better version of yourself. You will be more vibrant and exude more positivity. Surrender to self-care and be more present.

Alejandra Fernandez is a natural overachiever. She was born in Spain, studied in the US and the UK, and worked in the European Parliament. Currently, she aids women political legislators to communicate and market their messages efficiently. Alejandra always advocates for self-love as the best recipe for guiding your success and transmitting your message. She has helped countless female politicians to embrace themselves in self-love as a powerful shield against negative press and a great propeller of their message.

Every aspect of your life deserves your attention and care—your family, your marriage, your friendships, your business, or your job—but remember that the main thing that connects all those is you. **You are the center**, the structure that you build everything through and on top of.

As those things evolve and you work to preserve, improve, and care for yourself, for what you can and have built, for your soul and your life, you need to make sure the structure and base that ties them all stays safe, cared for, and loved. Make this structure the base for everything you do, **base everything on self-love and care and the rest will follow**.

"Self-care means focusing on your mind as much as you focus on your body, having self-love as your purpose for everything you do."

Alejandra Fernandez

COMMUNICATIONS CONSULTANT
FOR THE WOMEN POLITICAL LEADERS
GLOBAL FORUM (WPL)

21 SELF-CARE

Valentina Hernandez Botero is a firm defender of the many definitions of the word *love*, one of them being changing your inner dialogue to one of accepting our bodies and loving who we are. After designing many brands throughout her career, she opened a skin care studio under this premise. The result is that her business radiates self-care from the moment you walk in. The concept is to train your skin to heal from within and that is her main idea behind self-love—to let yourself heal by caring and being kind toward yourself.

We are wired to hold ourselves accountable harder and less objectively than others. We judge our abilities, looks, and thoughts constantly and harder than we would anyone else. Why are we so rough on ourselves? As if life was not hard enough, **we are our own toughest critics**, bringing up points that others don't even notice. This all ends up being highly detrimental for our productivity and can cause stress and anxiety. So how can we combat it? By practicing self-compassion.

Self-compassion is the art of being just a little bit kinder to ourselves. Talk to yourself as you would to someone you care for and love. Speak softly with a warm heart and change negative words and thoughts into positive ideas and solutions. Don't be afraid of losing your discipline; being self-compassionate won't affect your willpower. If anything, you'll soften the importance of the critique, offering a more sympathetic, constructive feedback to yourself that will allow you to continue creating and growing without fearing judgment. **Grow**, **improve**, **and be kind to yourself**.

"*What we must strive for is deep content and self-knowledge. Change the dialogue toward ourselves from one of criticism to one of love and understanding.*"

Valentina Hernandez Botero

FOUNDER AND CHIEF BRAND OFFICER OF
SANA SKIN STUDIO AND CLEAN BEAUTY VISIONARY

Denise Focil found a way to express the many dimensions that we as women have through fashion design. The armor concept was part of her learnings as a designer in Italy for renowned motorcycle apparel brand Alpinestars. Alpinestars has been making iconic motorcycle leather jackets since the 1960s, and while designing for them, Denise discovered the beauty in protecting yourself with something that expresses who you are and how you feel at that particular moment.

As an icon of the fashion world, Denise encourages us to express self-love by empowering ourselves from the moment we get dressed. To use our clothes as the uniform and armor we need to get through challenges because, ultimately, don't we all feel amazing when we put on our favorite piece and say to ourselves: **Today I can take over anything**.

Our clothes are how we present ourselves not only to the world but also to our recorded self-image. While it can be time-consuming or even daunting to style outfits for the day, **remember that you will dress how you feel and feel what you are wearing**. It is often said that new sneakers can motivate you to take on a workout or a fancy suit will make you feel more present in a meeting. The reason is that we often associate uniforms with jobs or tasks and when we underdress or lack time to invest in curating our image, we might feel out of place or unprepared for some of the tasks we have to face. Call it therapy, call it uniform, call it a work of art, but dressing up is a fantastic method for self-expression and self-care.

"Clothing is our armor for the day. Why not dress the way we want our day to be? If you want to own the boardroom, dress for it. If you want to have fun, dress for it. A successful day starts in your closet."

Denise Focil

FOUNDER AND DESIGNER OF AS BY DF AND ASTARS, AND CREATOR OF THE PERFECT LEATHER JACKET

Sofia Gutierrez de la Garza is a talented flower arrangement designer and creative boss girl that sees flowers as a way to express her feelings. Her arrangements are irregular and never symmetric, and they feature different flower types and a variety of colors. Even when something in her work doesn't seem perfect, she forgives the imperfections and continues working on her arrangements, giving herself the space to innovate because once those flowers come together, they become a beautiful representation of her emotional state. Self-love allows us to have compassion for ourselves and be kind when we need it the most, which results in a beautiful outcome.

When facing a situation that requires you to start over, to gather the strength to build something from scratch—whether it's a company or a new project you are working on—you will need to **give yourself more leeway than usual to make mistakes** and to exercise failures without big consequences in order to foment innovation and allow for more self-love to incite creativity.

Perfectionism is a revered concept in our society; it is the highest peak, the unattainable, and we all aspire to it. However, have you tried to work or think of something as if you had a safety net below you? Wouldn't you be more open to new ideas and perhaps bolder moves if you knew perfectionism does not exist and is not a realistic goal? **Release the boundaries of what is expected and think outside the box**; moreover, think as if there were no box at all, no wrong answers. **Love yourself for trying and encourage yourself to continue**. This is the basis of self-love; this is the basis of success.

"When starting something new, you have to be vulnerable, have self-compassion, and let go of perfectionism to achieve the space you need to create and innovate."

Sofia Gutierrez de la Garza

FOUNDER OF ANTHOS FLORAL STUDIO
AND FLOWER ARTIST

24 SELF-CARE

Della Heiman is a Harvard graduate in a relentless pursuit to transform her community through plant-based foods served in casual settings and for a mainstream audience. Her ventures changed the food landscape in Miami when she opened the first collaborative space there, in order to build a community around food in Miami's Wynwood district. Since then she has invested in educating thousands on the benefits of clean eats.

Della understood early on about the importance of food, how it not only serves as a very natural way to connect with each other as humans, but also as a way to heal ourselves from the inside. She is an advocate of listening to the unique needs and demands of your body to fuel your growth with wholesome nutrients.

Your body is the vessel in which your mind and soul travel, and it is the single most important thing for you to take care of. It works like a machine of sorts, creating and developing from the energy you put into it. Because of this, it is imperative to listen to your needs—**your body understands its needs and will speak to you if you listen carefully**. Treat it like a temple, understand the effects that different nutrients have on your temple, and take care of its health above all. If you do so, you will feel reenergized and have the strength to take on the day.

"Your body
is graced with ancient,
intuitive wisdom. She loves
when you listen to her honestly
and humbly, and fuel her with
clean, nourishing eats."

Della Heiman

FOUNDER OF DELLA
BOWLS, AND
YARD HOSPITALITY,
MIAMI'S FIRST
CULINARY INCUBATOR

4 SELF-CARE

After having many successful leadership roles in Fortune 500 companies, Gerri Sapinoso Hudson came to understand how important it is to practice self-care techniques like meditation daily. She studied at the Search Inside Yourself Leadership Institute (SIYLI), a Google spin-off dedicated to understanding the benefits of meditation for improving one's well-being. She learned that meditation has many physical and mental health benefits, from reducing stress and anxiety to connecting you with your inner self and increasing self-awareness. She discovered that meditation was a form of showing yourself love. Meditation has not only improved her life and understanding of herself but also improved her performance as a business leader.

You deserve to be pampered and loved; working yourself to exhaustion is not going to make you happy or successful in the long run. **The basis of success is a happy and healthy lifestyle** that you will have to purposely make time for and turn into a habit. The world moves faster every day, and our bodies and minds cannot keep up with the pace we must face. Making time to intentionally stop and meditate will reinvigorate you and **allow you to connect with the deepest, most vulnerable parts of yourself and strengthen them**.

Take time to meditate for five minutes each day. Remind yourself that there are 1,440 minutes in one day and you need to allocate just five to meditation. Once you practice this for three weeks, it will become a habit. You can increase the time and add more activities as you go. You will start to see how such **a small self-care act can have such a big impact in your life**.

"Meditation is the first step in self-care. You can connect with yourself in just one breath. In that stillness, you open your eyes to a world in which anything is possible, shift to gratitude, and all the obstacles to caring for yourself just melt away."

Gerri Sapinoso Hudson

MEDITATION FACILITATOR
AND PERSONAL LEADERSHIP COACH

Kelsey Zamoyski founded her business, Defy Therapy and Wellness, to give people the opportunity to heal themselves after an injury or physical flaw. Many of her clients have avoided surgery thanks to her treatment methods. One of the main elements of the Defy Therapy process is the daily at-home exercise routine that is meant to heal and strengthen your body. Kelsey has found that routinely doing something positive for your body can prevent further injuries and allow you to heal on your own.

Committing to healthy routines is a wonderful way to ensure that you are dedicating enough time to your overall well-being. **Start by creating a simple mindful routine, morning and night**. A great morning ritual could feature things like five minutes of meditation, setting an intention for the day, repeating a mantra, practicing yoga, stretching or doing a short workout, going for a run or walk, drinking your morning beverage by the window or on your favorite chair, enjoying a few minutes of silence, and a healthy breakfast.

A sample night ritual can include a warm drink without caffeine—preferably something soothing—applying a sheet face mask or other night treatment, practicing gratitude for the day and the path you are on, reading a book, and listening to soothing sounds or music. The most important thing is that anything that becomes part of your routine is geared toward better sleep and waking up rested and rejuvenated. If that means preparing some things for the day ahead so you can sleep a bit longer, then so be it. **Girl, you need that beauty sleep!**

"YOUR BODY CAN AND WILL HEAL; COMMIT TO HEALTH."

Kelsey Zamoyski

FOUNDER OF DEFY THERAPY
AND WELLNESS, AND RENOWNED
OCCUPATIONAL THERAPIST

4 SELF-CARE

Linda Parra is a big promoter of the importance of self-care in order to keep yourself at your best and preserve your identity beyond those you care for. Linda's point for this is simple: While she wears many hats, she knows that titles don't define who you are; you are you before you are anything else. Taking care of you is important, so that you can wear all the hats. She has established a few keys to achieving the balance of self-care and love she needs. For example, every Wednesday she hosts friends for dinner. She has her calendar marked with weekly visits to the spa, exercising, and philanthropy and charity work at the Wild and Whimsy Foster Care Foundation. Linda also makes time for dates with the hubby and makes sure not to neglect any of her weekly appointments, because consistency is key to keeping up with self-care.

Make a point of carving out time for yourself, and invest in disconnecting and recharging. The stressors of daily life need to be compensated for a self-care routine that will allow you to reenergize. The change doesn't have to be a big departure from your current activities. Instead, start by including small periods of time in your daily schedule or kids' routine for yourself. Dedicate these periods to things you enjoy, things that bring you peace of mind and are beneficial for your body, mind, and soul.

Being rested, cared for, and a priority to yourself will allow you to put out the best version of yourself. **You will exude love and joy**.

"Being a mother is the hat I wear the proudest, but one day my children will start their own families, and I need to have my own life outside of them. Therefore, I work. I work on my marriage, my friendships, my businesses, my mind, and my body. I make sure my kids are happy, healthy, and cared for, but I also make sure I take care of myself."

Linda Parra

MOM, DOCTOR, DENTAL CLINIC OWNER, AND WILD AND WHIMSY FOSTER CHILDREN FOUNDATION ADVOCATE

When Liv Albert prepares her podcast episodes, she associates it with the current events that are happening and amazes everyone by showing us how much we can learn from texts that were composed thousands of years ago. She is a constant reminder that it is our history that brought us all the advances and changed the future to what we experience today. She uses her love for learning and history to connect us to the present and future. Part of self-care and love is to continue growing not only your body and soul, but also your mind. The moment that we stop learning or cultivating ourselves, we are losing touch with history, our contemporary context, and our mental stimulation.

It is a crucial part of self-care to continue educating ourselves. How else would we understand our current situation and be prepared for the future? A mind that is not stimulated through reading and learning is a mind that is left to just unilaterally absorb the information that other mediums offer, and usually that comes with a lot of advertising and what we can call junk media. There is something about getting lost in a book about anything and everything that might interest you and inspires creativity.

Learning and reading have so many positive side effects and can make you a more interesting dinner guest, too! Set a goal of learning a certain amount of things every month or reading about three topics by the end of the month; you will feel accomplished and might even discover a new passion for something. **So, what is next on your reading list?**

"READING ABOUT, LEARNING FROM, AND CRITIQUING THE PAST IS HOW WE CREATE AN AMAZING FUTURE."

Liv Albert

CREATOR OF THE PODCAST
LET'S TALK ABOUT MYTHS, BABY!
AND HISTORY LOVER

Kasey Dixon is a woman who wears many hats—entrepreneur, interior decorator, blogger, and farmhouse owner, among others. Don't mistake her for a full-time country girl though—she was once was once an LA city girl who worked for a big fashion corporation before she decided she was ready for a slower pace of life to invest in her own self-care. She chose to dedicate her time to those things that truly made her happy, like remodeling a beautiful modern farmhouse in Idaho.

Four years after remodeling her farmhouse, she became pregnant and in preparation for her growing family she looked for joy in creating a new, larger space to prepare for her new adventure. She knew this would be a lot of work, but she needed this to continue her path to happiness and self-love. Within a short span of time, she sold the farmhouse at a great profit and moved to start another beautiful remodel story. How fantastic is that? It is the very example of setting an intention, investing in our well-being and happiness, and then having the universe manifest bountifully.

There are so many wonderful and positive side effects to making a choice for your own happiness, for yourself. These decisions should never be shamed as selfish, because **investing in yourself will present huge benefits in the long run**. It's a purposeful choice you're making, and unknowingly you're receiving back so much more, because you're able to create much more when **you're in a place of comfort and joy**.

"Self-love and care are where it all starts. If you don't take time for yourself, everything else will suffer. Create space for the things that bring you joy!"

Kasey Dixon

FOUNDER OF BOOZIE,
SBK LIVING, AND LIFESTYLE BLOGGER

5

HAPPINESS

IN THE PURSUIT OF HAPPINESS.

(LIVE IN THE MOMENT.)

We are all in search of happiness. At times, it can seem like we will never be able to be happy or at least as happy as we would like to be. The thing is that happiness is a choice. We decide how we want to live. We can choose to be happy or let sadness take over our lives.

We will inevitably encounter sad moments in our lives that will prevent us from being happy at one moment in time, but difficult times do pass. Allow yourself to heal from situations that caused a great deal of pain. Forgive who you hurt you, let go of control, move toward a better future. Don't hold on to things that are toxic to your well-being, even if it means letting go of someone you love.

Do more things that make you feel passionate. Is there something that you always wanted to try? Do it. Pursue that dream even if it seems far-fetched. You will never get there if you don't try. Being happy is about making choices even if it scares us. Little choices lead us one step closer to our goals.

Learn to say "no" to people and situations that may not serve you. There's always something you may not want to do, but you do it anyway for someone you love, and that's okay. Then there are things we do that drain our energy and make us feel worse at the end of the day. Practice saying "no" to things that drain your energy or causes you stress. Find peace in saying it and give that word power in your vocabulary. Don't feel bad about doing what is best for you and your mental health.

Then, practice saying "yes" to things that light you up inside—the things that make you feel alive, like you have a purpose in life. Say "yes" more to the things that make you smile and help you forget the number of hours in a day. Don't waste a moment doing something you don't want to do. Spend time on things that make you feel joy. You will see that once you give space to what serves you and let go of what doesn't, great things will come your way.

If you don't know what makes you happy, take a few minutes each day to explore small things, like spending some more time with your family, or spending time outdoors and breathing in the fresh air. Search for things you have never done before, like taking a painting class or going bungee jumping. It doesn't have to be something big or out of this world; just find time to explore your likes and dislikes.

Recall a time when you felt happy or a happy memory. Whenever you feel your thoughts starting to enter a negative spiral, remember that time in your life and refocus your thoughts. Take time to be thankful for your happy memories and the good things that life has to offer. Practice daily gratitude to reframe your thinking into one of joy. Happiness is available to you at any time. Find things that you are grateful for each day, even if it's as simple as being alive.

Find the time to get to know yourself, take in the little moments in life, discover the charm in the day, and happiness will follow.

5 HAPPINESS

I used to find my mind wondering about future situations, conditioning my happiness to things or events that may or may not happen. Once I reached my goals, that was never enough; another thought would come up with an ever-more ambitious feat ahead, leaving me trapped in a never-ending circle where happiness, the ultimate goal, was never achieved. Feeling lost and not knowing what step to take next in order to achieve happiness is a common feeling. Instinctively, we might cling to an idea that our happiness is determined by a person or a situation, and this then limits our opportunity to act on it, leaving us paralyzed and helpless.

Reframe your happiness as an individual goal and own where you are and how you feel. This is a product of your decisions and changing your life is just a step away, but it requires commitment and intent. **Explore the things that make you happy and those that don't**. Release yourself from the moments that bring you down and increase those that motivate you and make you want to smile. I started by making a list of all the things that I currently have that make me happy and that I'm grateful for and I made it a goal to be present, to be aware, and to understand why this situation, at this moment, with these people, is exactly where I needed to be.

Only once you are happy can you share this gift with others; you cannot blame others for your situation, and others shouldn't expect you to make them happy when they cannot do it for themselves. When following this premise, relationships are healthier, and love is abundant and true, based on fairness and responsibility.

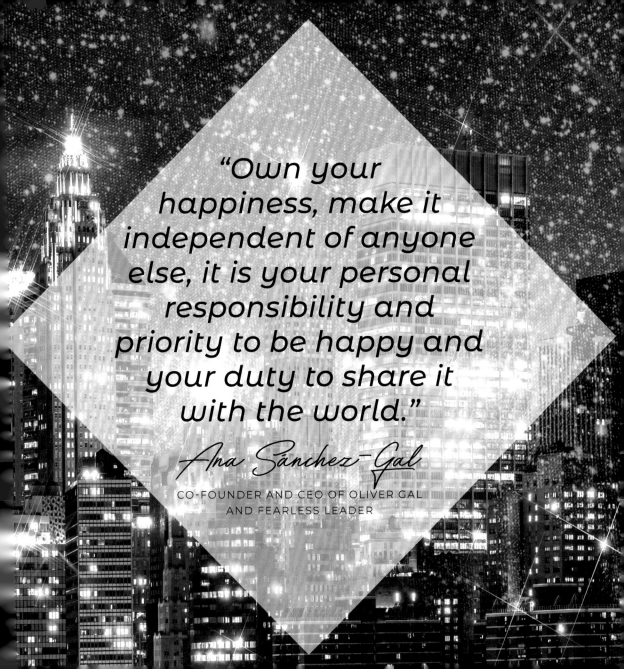

"Own your happiness, make it independent of anyone else, it is your personal responsibility and priority to be happy and your duty to share it with the world."

Ana Sánchez-Gal

CO-FOUNDER AND CEO OF OLIVER GAL
AND FEARLESS LEADER

5 HAPPINESS

Soledad Picón is a staple of the philanthropic and art communities in South Florida and Latin America. While she was always a leading force in strategic marketing and PR through her company Picón & Co., and brought about many achievements while on the board of directors of major organizations, she only truly found happiness when she was able to apply her skills to improving the community and raising funds for charitable purposes related to women. This wasn't easy, it required effort, passion, and a lot of creativity, but it was rewarding beyond belief.

Since then, Soledad has shared with the world the unwavering belief **in the power of giving back to inspire and change lives**. Because of this, she truly believes that happiness is a conscious decision we make that takes real effort. She is involved in so many ventures, including being the chair of Women United of United Way of Miami-Dade and in the Bass Museum of Art Development Committee. It is through all of these projects that she creates her happiness, which is the source of her motivation to continue pushing.

The truth is that by **finding happiness in our lives and choosing it over greed, sadness, or negativity will we be able to see that there is positivity in everything**, and that will help us surpass obstacles that may come our way.

"Happiness is a choice that takes effort, passion, and a lot of creativity ... and still is the simplest thing to achieve."

Soledad Picón

PHILANTHROPIST, SOCIAL IMPACT & STRATEGIC PARTNERSHIPS EXECUTIVE

113

5 HAPPINESS

Jennifer DiMotta is a fierce, overachieving woman who has had the opportunity to lead many teams during her career. As an e-commerce expert, she has taken many brands that are considered ubiquitous from relative anonymity to direct-to-consumer stardom. She has proven that she is unafraid to take on new challenges. She learned that in order to be able to make bold moves and achieve something great, you must let go of relationships or situations that set you back, and she has made it a point to surround herself with those who complete her. She inspires others to leverage the power of teamwork to achieve their goals, to understand that their own happiness is above everything, because one's success is conditioned by it.

Take a minute and think about your past month. How much time have you dedicated to people who make you happy, bring you joy, and help you on your path toward happiness versus people who drain your energy and make you feel depleted? **We are who we surround ourselves with**; those in our circle share their energy with us and generate vibrations that reverberate onto us. Stop exposing yourself to toxic people.

You are worthy of a wonderful circle of friends, of an incredible and supportive team, of having peace of mind and positivity around you. There is no guilt at leaving behind toxic people; it will only help them realize what they're missing and lead you on a better path.

"A desire to be around others who fill in your gaps or help smooth out your high and low points has been a very successful strategy for me. When I'm practical, disciplined, and determined to make it happen, and then I leverage the power of teamwork, success and happiness have always followed."

Jennifer DiMotta

OWNER OF DIMOTTA CONSULTING, LLC,
FEMALE LEADERSHIP EVANGELIST,
AND AWARD-WINNING SPEAKER

5 HAPPINESS

Happiness is sometimes described as being satisfied, being grateful and proud of where you are, when, and with whom. It is the ultimate goal to be happy in our lives, especially with what we do daily. While Nan Lindesmith enjoyed being a nurse practitioner, she yearned for more and made the decision to take up what truly made her happy—decorating and blogging about interior design. She always had a natural talent for creating spaces that were styled to perfection. She started sharing images of her own home's decorating projects and gained an amazing following overnight, because of the simplicity and glamour of her designs.

It is important to ask ourselves periodically: **Am I following my passion? Is this something I truly love? Does this make me genuinely happy?** Because only when you follow your passion and really dig into what it is that makes your heart race and your brain feel like you want days to have more hours—because you'd like to keep on doing that forever—can you achieve happiness. The best part? When doing what you love, work becomes a hobby, an everlasting interest that gives you purpose and that generates happiness—and with time, those dreams you never knew could come true will become your reality. **Materialize your dreams by committing to happiness and following your passion**.

Remember to ask yourself: If money wasn't an issue, or if my situation was any other, would I be doing this still? Is this what I'd like to pursue? **Look for happiness in every little thing you do every day**.

"LIVE A LIFE IN 'PINK'—FOLLOW PASSIONS THAT IGNITE WHAT YOU NEVER KNEW COULD COME TRUE!"

Nan Lindesmith

FOUNDER OF NANLINDY
AND DREAM INTERIOR CREATOR

5 HAPPINESS

Nicole Thaw is one of those beautiful souls who was looking for happiness in material things, unfulfilling jobs, and superficial relationships even though she is an extremely intelligent and spiritual soul who craved meaning. She just didn't know it at the time. When she found breathwork, she found how to bring all her negative thoughts into a state of consciousness where she could act on them and get on a powerful transformational path toward happiness.

Nicole discovered the power of the breath on a solo trip to Bali, where she took her first class in breathwork and discovered that breath holds the power to transform one's life. **When you change what's inside, everything around you starts changing and happiness becomes easily attainable**. She felt a profound change in her emotional, mental, and physical condition from her experience and found happiness in taking everything she learned along her journey and sharing it with the world. She realized that the power to succeed and attain joy was inside of her all along. When she is performing this transformational technique, she doesn't require any more tools than the power of her soul to guide another through the class.

We frequently find ourselves looking for happiness in others, in remote places, in events that are outside of our control. However, Nicole is a wonderful example of how happiness can be found within and how it will make you unstoppable. A true force of nature.

"The greatest life lesson I have learned through my journey back to myself is that the power lies, and has always laid, within yourself to find happiness. You, and only you, have the power in any moment to create and manifest a life beyond your wildest dreams. When you reconnect with that power, you become a woman who runs with wolves."

Nicole Thaw

FOUNDER OF MOON BREATH
AND BREATHWORK FACILITATOR

5 HAPPINESS

When working on her innovative salon concept, María Camila Piedrahita experienced many setbacks that made her rethink the whole possibility of opening her business. Instead of drowning in despair, she remained optimistic and grateful, always hopeful that her hard work would lead to something great. She was compassionate with herself and knew that she would reach her objective eventually as long as she kept going. Today, her company, Blow to Paris, is a successful salon concept with thousands of customers and a founder who knows that happiness is right around the corner.

We are by nature defined by duality: we desire certain things but at the same time don't expect them because the context or other factors make us think they're unattainable. We love something, but we don't truly believe we're worthy enough to have it. We aspire to be something, but we don't take the right steps to get there. In order to find harmony in this duality, we can practice the law of attraction. In summary, this theory says you will receive that which you radiate.

It's simple: **you are energy and it flows through you**. When you are present and mindful, and consciously make the decision to be optimistic and positive, even when you are thrown a curveball, you can be a better version of you and see beyond your problems. You are then able to focus on something greater, the next thing that you are attracting with your positivity—**your true destiny**. Don't focus on your fears and what you can lose; focus on being positive, mindful, and present and a greater good will come to you. **How will you be more positive today?**

"Be grateful, be present, be optimistic, be compassionate. Maybe you don't see it now, but happiness is right around the corner!"

Maria Camila Piedrahita

FOUNDER AND CEO
OF BLOW TO PARIS

5 HAPPINESS

Jessica Motes faced many critics when starting her business. They wondered how she could ever make a success of baking and selling vegan chocolate chip cookies. It seemed like continuing her successful career as a model would have been the natural path for her to take, but she wasn't fulfilled. She was ready for something new and exciting. Like many creative and entrepreneurial people, it took her a while to pick a path—she's talented at many things—but once she shared those mouth-melting, happiness-inducing cookies with the world, the verdict was clear. She was going to be America's vegan cookie queen—and she finally found something that not only made her successful but also made her wildly happy, because while you can be good at many things, **you should truly pick those things that you really enjoy doing, that you love**.

Taking part in something that you truly enjoy can help you overcome the toughest situations and become the best version of yourself. A dedicated and passionate woman can take any situation and make a positive outcome out of it; it is entirely up to you. However, isn't it much sweeter to do it when you truly love what you do? It is easy to fall back on the comfort of what we know and what we are used to, our good ol' habits. But **what if you took a step towards your happiness**; **what would you gain?** How much happier would you be?

You are the only one standing in the way of a happier future, and it's that one decision that can change everything. **Take the plunge, do the thing, change your life**—after all, it's yours.

"DOING WHAT YOU LOVE MAKES LIFE THAT MUCH HAPPIER AND SWEETER!"

Jessica Motes

FOUNDER OF THE NAUGHTY COOKIE
AND VEGAN COOKIE QUEEN

5 HAPPINESS

Shayna Hasson found yoga after suffering from stress, anxiety, and lower back pain. This is what brought her to eventually open her business and what has allowed her to become a yoga expert around the world. She overcame her struggles and persevered to the point of changing her career and life. Everything we feel and experience is composed of two parts, two opposites that make a whole. How could we acknowledge happiness and the true feeling of joy if we are not aware of what it is to be void of it? Being mindful and investing time in understanding your situation and context is a truly useful way to be present and really appreciate "good times." Shayna found true happiness leaving the busy restaurant industry and turning to yoga.

Remember an unpleasant situation that you have overcome or left behind. You have persevered and risen above that to get to today. **Be proud of yourself**. You chose happiness and succeeded. You chose joy and can now appreciate it. Life, as the eternal teacher, will guide our journeys through ups and downs, hindrances, and difficulties, and while we need to accept this, we should also consider it a rather positive thing.

Setbacks are often a wonderful learning experience. Think about it: it is way more satisfying to gain a victory after a long streak of losses. That is why it's important to enjoy every loss. **Use every failure as an opportunity to learn from experience**, to understand yourself better, and to prepare for happiness, for success, for victory, and for joy.

"Be present every day,
not just in happiness and success
but in sadness, struggles,
and failures. Why? Because
it's those exact struggles that
make the success so sweet."

Shayna Hasson

OWNER AND CEO OF YOGA BEYOND THE STUDIO

5 HAPPINESS

Michaela Nessim, an artist of Jamaican and Swedish descent, found her well of inspiration by accepting her origins as a unique gift and letting go of comparison. She used her heritage to express herself through her work by sharing beautiful, captivating images with the world. How incredibly special it is to be different in some way. It is the most wonderful gift you have been blessed with, and if instead of seeing it as a negative discrepancy with the norm, you own it and welcome it, then you can use this as a special tool to create, to find joy, and to produce works that spark joy in others too.

Social media makes comparison inevitable, and inadvertently it can bring us down when the ideals that society highlights differ from the attributes we've been blessed with. It is normal and nothing to be ashamed of, but when this happens, **do not let comparison steal your happiness and tarnish your joy.** Instead, look for what makes you different and make it a challenge to exploit that in a way that can make you happy, that can help you reach your goals, achieve success, and feel loved.

From all the gifts you've been blessed with that make you different and unique, **which one will you use to create something?**

"You can tap into your own strength by first owning who you are. You hold the key to your own happiness; harness the power of authenticity and let go of comparison."

Michaela Nessim

MOM, OIL PAINTING VIRTUOSO, AND FANTASY WORLD CREATOR

5 HAPPINESS

Despite studying marine biology, Jenny Rey felt like her soul needed creativity and changed a biology career for the pursuit of hairstyling. Over ten years later, she is a renowned celebrity stylist and an educator in the field. Doing this fills her mind with ideas and heart with joy, and she wouldn't change it for anything else. There is nothing more exhilarating than going to bed thinking about the excitement of doing something you love the next day. Of wanting the day to have more hours just so you can continue with something because it fills you with so much thrill and makes you truly happy!

Finding happiness in creative activities is a wonderful way to develop our most advanced power—the power to create and change reality so that it can manifest our dreams and produce happiness and beauty around us. This is a gift that has been bestowed upon us and should be exploited to achieve happiness within ourselves, but also to gift happiness to others.

Think of those things that make you want to jump out of your bed, that allow you to sleep like a baby with a smile on your face, or that motivate you to do the impossible and excite you to sail ahead. Those are the things that make you happy; they are the ones that bring love, purpose, and peace to your life. **The things that bring you joy are the ones you should pursue and protect**. Identify them and look for what ignites you in every single thing that you do, because after all, living a life of peace and purpose is the perfect way to ensure happiness and love.

"Creativity and happiness are two things that can't exist one without the other. When you feed your creativity, you feed your soul, and that in return creates happiness. Nothing worth doing comes easy, but the outcome is euphoric."

Jenny Rey

HAIR CREATIVE,
BIOLAGE AMBASSADOR,
AND EDUCATOR

6
CREATIVITY

MAKE MAGIC HAPPEN.

(INSPIRE. INNOVATE. CREATE.)

Creativity is where all the magic happens. It is the window to our soul and the deepest parts of us. It's the child within us that allows us to imagine and explore the wonder that is life. It's the place where we can connect with the inner part of us and discover who we are.

Creativity lets us be who we want to be without fearing judgment. What are some things that you do creatively? If you don't have an answer, then it's time to uncover that part of yourself and let yourself be free. Don't let the fear of being judged stop you from doing your best work. Just have fun and let yourself be carried away by that part of you.

It is not a competition or a race to see who can innovate the most or who has the better ideas. It's about being vulnerable and letting yourself make mistakes. Art is liberating and teaches us to find the greatness in the mistakes, to use the lessons, to experiment, to learn, to grow. Sometimes art can take us to dark places, but in the end, it leads us to the light inside of us, waiting to ignite.

Being creative is not about being perfect. It is about the imperfections. It leads us to our passions and helps us discover who we are. Start now, use whatever you have without fear, and create art. It doesn't have to be a painting or a drawing; it can be anything that you consider to be art, from dancing to writing to creating a new idea. Let the possibilities fly without expectation.

Don't think too much about it. Don't expect anything. Don't judge it. Just let it flow. The more you use it, the more confident you will be in yourself. Imagination takes courage and it is everything. It leads to inspiration, innovation, and the creation of new and unique things. It leads to discoveries we never thought possible. It takes creativity to be able to see things from different perspectives and come up with distinct ideas. Without a little bit of imagination, we would be stuck in a world of impossibilities.

Let your creativity put your imagination into action. Let it lead you to find new ways to connect with people and design new projects. We can't develop amazing things without using our creative magic. It requires passion, and passion helps us discover what makes us happy. Needless to say, we can't find joy without a little bit of creativity. It can seem like creativity doesn't come as naturally to you as it may come to others, but everyone can learn to be creative. All it takes is a little practice. Think of the people you find to be great innovators; what made them so? What creative things did they come up with? A new invention? A new system? How can you use your creative skills to innovate?

Creativity inspires, and you are an inspiration. Use your talents to make the impossible happen. Remember, imagination and creativity lie within you. You just have to find it. Find the color in your world and use that to transform your ideas. Turn your dreams into reality.

6 CREATIVITY

Katy Hirschfeld uses art as a way to express her feelings to make a powerful social commentary on reality. Her art pieces often represent colorful collaged faces of women who are challenging the status quo and have hidden messages throughout their skin. This makes Katy's creations completely intimate. Her work is a reflection of her feelings and the path she chose to express her thoughts. While she can come across as standoffish when you first meet her, because of her shyness, her art exposes her kind soul and genius to the world, breaking down the walls she has and her difficulties with becoming close to people, truly changing the perception you can have of her.

There is no deeper place, more vulnerable spot, than the one in your soul that produces art. As if it were magic, **creativity exposes the raw part of you**. You experience an intimate exchange with your art. Your artwork or creative project can be a way of taking down the hard shells and walls around you. Art has a mind of its own. It spells inspiration and leads us to create things that sometimes we even wonder whether we could recreate when lost.

Creativity can be used in a million ways, for the most precise to the wildest tasks, and to create many different things. This is a present we need to share with the world because art is everywhere, but it lies in the eye of the beholder, so when you share your creativity with another person, with your kids, with your loved ones, **you are giving them your unique perspective of the world**, a gift that only you can give them.

"THE MOST RAW
AND INTIMATE
PLACE OF ONESELF
IS CREATIVITY."

Katy Hirschfeld

AWARD-WINNING ARTIST AND
FEMINISM ADVOCATE
THROUGH COLLAGE

6 CREATIVITY

While studying political economy at Georgetown, Luisa Santos discovered the potential of nitrogen to create ice cream and decided to test it out in several pop-up events. While nitrogen ice cream was quite a novelty and this was beyond her field of knowledge, she continued experimenting until she founded Lulu's and brought it back to her hometown of Miami.

The question is: **What happens when we don't think of ourselves as creative types?** Have you ever told yourself: There's just not another solution to this problem, I'll never think of it, when you are invoking the goddess in you to provide the inspiration while at the same time starting the task and diligently working on it.

Continuous practice will improve any brainstorming or creative session. Look beyond the main idea in your mind right now; **exercise introspection and truly release your feelings and thoughts** about the subject at hand. Practice just writing it out, scribbling or depicting these thoughts, as if there were **no constraints**, **no filters, no limits**. In that exercise, in those notes, you will find your most creative self: the deepest aspects of your mind and the reflection of the power of your subconscious, which goes beyond the obvious to produce truly brilliant and unique ideas. You have just commenced a cycle of continuous improvement that will make you feel like your latest creation is the best to date.

"You'll never get it perfect the first time but starting somewhere will force you into a cycle of improvement."

Luisa Santos

FOUNDER OF
LULU'S ICE CREAM AND
NITROGEN ICE CREAM SCIENTIST

6 CREATIVITY

Pily Montiel studied psychology and thought that it would lead her to a career in the field, but instead she ended up following her love of fashion design and creativity to become a renowned fashion illustrator and design icon. While studying the wonders of the mind, she realized that many of the ailments that our society suffers from could be healed through creativity. She applied this theory to herself when she started her illustration and design studio, finding that her soul was free of worries and at her happiest when she was creating.

Using creativity to channel your emotions and release tensions is a technique that, while it might take a little bit to get used to, is one of the best healing practices you can engage in. Start by finding a medium through which you can express your feelings. **Don't limit your creativity to art or painting**; it can be done in any form of creation—it could be singing, dancing, or writing.

Once you choose your medium, let your feelings flow; let them take over your mind and release all thoughts in your creation. When you're done, take a break and admire your creativity after a few hours, and **you will find aspects of yourself that you didn't see before**. You will see the result of many exploding feelings being reorganized into a new concept, a concept that will make others feel something, a work of beauty, a work of art.

"A creative mind channels emotions through creating and turning even sadness into beauty."

Pily Montiel

FASHION DESIGN VISIONARY,
SUSTAINABLE FASHION ADVOCATE,
AND RENOWNED ILLUSTRATOR

6 CREATIVITY

Federika Longinotti Buitoni's story is one that combines thoughtful curation with the appeal of creativity and doing things differently. Her appreciation for curation as a way to express her creativity started early on. Her mother is an architect, and during her upbringing her home was filled with antiques, design-driven furniture, and beautiful accent pieces.

Federika has grown up to be a talented entrepreneur, and this gave her the ability to let her imagination soar while being able to make her achievements a reality. This led to her conceiving Collecto, a revolutionary wedding registry where couples can find a curated selection of items in which each piece shares an intrinsic sense of craftsmanship, heritage, and design. Where others saw long and predictable wedding gift lists, Federika saw objects that told stories.

We find ourselves constantly presented with options, hundreds of them, all different, and we don't always have an easy way to sort or filter through them to choose the one that will bring us the most satisfaction. That is when we have to **resort to creativity to help us choose and discern through the many options we are given** to make something completely customized for us.

Next time you have to make a choice, **find a creative way to explain why that is what you chose**, and find the attributes that make it truly special to you. This will lead to a happier result and not just mindless consumption.

"In a world that is overflowing with options, curation and a creative spark are strongly influencing the experiences we desire. A curation with a distinctive point of view, paired with a creative angle that gives it an edge, is so much more powerful."

Federika Longinotti Buitoni

ENTREPRENEUR AND
FOUNDER OF COLLECTO

6 CREATIVITY

Alisa Ueno is a true renaissance woman; she is a patron of the arts, fashion, and music, and a recognized ambassador of the well-known art of partying. She travels the world looking for experiences, inspiration, and, most of all, remarkable moments, which she collects. Her goal is to continue building these memories, to make every second count—from DJing in Tokyo, to recording a top-charted song alongside Sofi Tukker and Nervo, all while modeling and directing her fashion brand, Fig and Viper. She is a great example of making it truly interesting by being wildly creative.

What will your family, your friends, your descendants say about you, long after you are gone? What stories will they tell, what example will you set, how far will you get? Will you be in their history? Will you be proud of your story? Will it be interesting? Unique? Creative? Bold?

Well, the good news is you still have plenty of time to make your mark and live up to your own expectations and make a difference in other people's lives. However, you must start now by being different, by thinking outside the box, by exploring your artistic side and applying it to your life. Nothing productive comes from being inactive. And nothing bold happens from repeating our actions, **so get creative and make it epic**.

"When making decisions, ask yourself, 'If I were to write my autobiography ten years from now, what should I do to make it an interesting story?'"

Alisa Ueno

CREATIVE DIRECTOR OF FIG AND VIPER,
DJ, MODEL, SINGER, AND TOKYO IT-GIRL

6 CREATIVITY

Deanna Weise's talent for art gets applied to everything she does. She has gone from being a DJ to being an illustrator, to being a travel blogger, and even food truck designer. She expresses her art in any way she can no matter what it is that she is doing. Deanna finds beauty and inspiration in everything around her, and in turn, transforms what she sees into a form of art.

As you are going about your day, stop and pay attention to what is around you. What does it look like? Did anything, in particular, make you smile today? **How did you experience beauty today?** There is beauty in absolutely everything, from human-made designs to the nature around us, and this beauty is the source of creativity.

As artists, we look for beauty in the small things, the things that make us smile. It might be the way glass reflects light in the middle of the afternoon or the last remains of a rainbow in a rainy traffic jam. **You have the power within you to look and find magnificence in everything**. Look at whatever is in front of you—what is charming about it, how is it different, and what makes it special? By exercising this, you will become aware of your surroundings, in touch with your environment, and more grateful for what you have. This will generate happiness, joy, and curiosity, all the secrets to living a creative life.

"The best kind of inspiration is to explore and see the world around you. It doesn't have to be far. Whether it's witnessing the Northern Lights in Iceland or people-watching at a local park, you'll realize once you fully immerse in the presence of being, the world has so much beauty to offer. And that should be the fuel you can use to create what you want to give back to the world."

Deanna Weise

GRAPHIC DESIGNER,
EXPERIENCE COLLECTOR, AND DOODLER

6 CREATIVITY

Nadine Ghosn's genius never fit the standard. Her innovative talent and new ways of approaching things have always defined everything she touches. After graduating from Stanford University, majoring in both art and economics, Nadine continued her corporate experience in the luxury industry for major brands like Hermès. This experience fueled her passion for jewelry and understanding of high-end craftsmanship. However, after breaking away from the tradition that often goes hand in hand with the luxury world and high-end jewelry brands, Nadine wanted to do something different, so she set off to make plain, ordinary products extraordinary through the art of jewelry design.

While our survival instincts might tell us to look for what we have in common, **it can be more interesting**, inspiring, and rewarding to look for what sets us apart, to be able to discover interesting aspects and unique abilities that differentiate us. That which makes each of us rare and special.

When you look at things, try to observe what is not obvious to anyone, put your touch through your enchanted vision tunnel and look at it in a different way. Once you can see the extraordinary in ordinary things, you will know that you have lit up your creative spark and you are ready to bathe in magic everything that you touch. **Find what makes you different and you'll find your secret power**.

"If you don't fit in, you are given a perspective that is unique to you. Use that to your advantage, because once you do, magic is on the horizon."

Nadine Ghosn

AWARD-WINNING JEWELRY DESIGNER,
UNLIMITED THINKER,
AND CREATOR

6 CREATIVITY

Creativity and storytelling are part of Jenny Mayberry's everyday work as a merchandiser. Throughout her career, she has found ways to create stories through the products she curates and collections she directs. She depicts stunning tales through the assortment of goods she merchandizes to captivate customers and create a visions made to inspire.

Explore the amazing wonders of creativity and the possibility of designing a beautiful world around you only by using your imagination and what you have within reach. There are so many things you can express through telling your story, or a lovely story can be a great way of using your talent.

Every art piece, every poem, song, installation, sculpture, or play are displays a story, a story that makes us feel and react, which never leaves us indifferent to it. That is what makes an artwork engaging and enchanting, the idea of producing something that provokes feelings of beauty and joy in the creator and the spectator.

Look around you, and observe and imagine how your house, your belongings, your creations, and your words are telling a story of who you are, your likes and dislikes, your aspirations, and all the good you have to share. **What does your art, your home, your work say about you? What story do they tell?**

"BEING CREATIVE IS TELLING A STORY. WHY NOT MAKE IT A BEAUTIFUL STORY?"

Jenny Mayberry
SENIOR MERCHANDISER AT
RESTORATION HARDWARE

6 CREATIVITY

When starting her company, Catherine Cu pivoted from building an art platform to designing tropical dental floss, through her and her sister's wildly successful company, Cocofloss. Catherine had worked as a financial analyst for some time when she decided to build an art commissioning platform. A few months into the project, with a lot of time and money invested in it, she realized that the world didn't need her art platform as much as they needed a better reason to floss. She kept an open mind and truly analyzed flossing. She and her sister researched the best material and ingredients to ensure the most amazing flossing experience; they reimagined dental floss as a glamorous part of daily self-care.

Catherine's flexibility enabled her to move from one concept to another, completely different one. She invested a great deal of time and effort in courageously and curiously looking at the real needs of the world and how to satisfy them with a product that feels new, luxurious, fancy, and cool.

Creativity is a key ingredient to reach success. Look at everything with a curious and truly naïve eye that will allow you to gather new conclusions and insight from the same things that everyone has around them. **Dedication, courage, and flexibility will allow a creative mind to flourish into success**. Look around you for opportunities, with an open and inquisitive mind, and you will find the world speaking back to you and uncovering overlooked chances and perhaps even your big break!

"Create something that the world really needs. To find this, carefully observe the world around you to uncover its secrets, test your ideas with customers as early as possible, and keep flexible. Entrepreneurship takes courage. You have to put your ideas out there for others to evaluate. But if you keep honest, flexible, and creative, you'll find your way to success."

Catherine Cu

CREATIVE CO-FOUNDER
AND CEO OF COCOFLOSS

6 CREATIVITY

Eda Men is a well-traveled and cultivated mind with the soul of an entrepreneur who can truly make things happen. As such, she has taken the reins and revolutionized her family's business as one of the world leaders in swimsuit and sportswear manufacturers. She never had a doubt; she understood the talent that we women have. **We are the ultimate creative beings.**

When starting her newest venture, a luxury swimwear brand, she wanted to make something that made women feel empowered. She realized that by designing pieces that were minimalistic but had interesting designs with flattering cuts and defining shapes to suit all body types, and that embraced true women, she had found the creative answer to highlighting women's confidence and power.

Eda found the answer to her quest through creativity and unleashing her imagination to find her **inner superpower**—the skill to design suits that will make women feel beautiful and inspired.

You have all the talent, strength, and ability to create and achieve your dreams, just because you're you—fierce and talented. You have overcome so many things and have created a life that is a strong part of yourself. Unleash your inner creativity, begin to explore all your talents, try something new. Everything you need is right here. **You are made of magic and the magic is inside of you.**

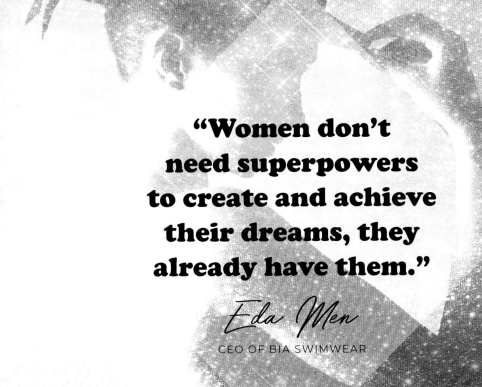

"Women don't need superpowers to create and achieve their dreams, they already have them."

Eda Men

CEO OF BIA SWIMWEAR

CONCLUSION

We hope that after reading this book you feel more inspired to take life on as the girl boss that you are. Go beyond your wildest imaginations and show the world your best self. You can achieve what you put your mind to, just believe in the power of you. Nobody is pionerfect and sometimes we will fail before we succeed, and that is okay! Things may not always happen as you want them to, but they will happen as they are meant to. Be kind to yourself and keep going on your journey of self-discovery. What is meant to be will find its way to you in due time. You are not in a race with anyone else but yourself.

Live in bravery and see the opportunities start coming your way. And by bravery, we don't mean doing all the big scary things you always feared of doing although that might be part of it for you! We mean taking those little steps every day to make your dreams come true even if you're afraid of what might happen next. If you want a new career, begin doing research into the career you want. Take action! The thing is that we never know what is going to happen in life especially if we don't try. Things are not set in stone and you always have the power to make a change for the better. A life well lived is all about continuing to take a chance on yourself.

Each woman featured in this book serves as a powerful reminder to tap into the courage that lives inside of you to live the life that you want. The women included in this book were chosen because their brilliant stories and remarkable careers are great examples of overcoming adversity. They are trailblazers that live in their bravery every day and show us that even our failures are possibilities to leading a future that we want. We encourage you to carry these women with you throughout your journey and use their aspirational advice to follow your path to happiness.

We know that it can sometimes be a challenging task to get through the day because there are times that we may lack the motivation to power through or there may be days when we don't feel like our best selves. But we truly hope that this book brings you joy, inspiration, and positivity to counter those days. Change a down day into a happy and productive one, into a constructive and learning one, into a loving and growing one, so you are living a life full of purpose. You will encounter difficult days but know that those hard days will pass, and you will find the light at the end of the tunnel again.

We always strive to be our best—our highs and lows are simply part of life and what we do. As entrepreneurs, the constant among all the noise that surrounds our life is the powerful belief that everything bad is just temporary and success and happiness are inevitable. When you keep this belief behind every one of your thoughts and actions, everything you do will contribute to achieving your goals and a beautiful life. After all, it is not by chance that this book ended up in your hands, it is because you are already pursuing these goals and the universe is conspiring to help you get there.

Lola & Ana

CONTRIBUTORS

ABOUT THE AUTHORS

Lola Sánchez Herrero is Chief Creative Officer of the internationally renowned lifestyle and art brand Oliver Gal. An acclaimed artist and successful entrepreneur, Sánchez Herrero is using her creativity, technical skill and business savvy to revolutionize the art and home decor industry with fresh products and compelling brands.

Sánchez Herrero started her career in 2006 as a designer and illustrator at AllPopArt, a customizable art company led by her sister Ana Sánchez-Gal. In 2012, Sánchez Herrero and Sánchez-Gal co-founded Oliver Gal Artist Co., where Sánchez Herrero currently leads the creative direction and Sánchez-Gal acts as the company's CEO. The success of their leadership is apparent: Oliver Gal products have been featured in many U.S. and international publications, including *Glamour*, *People*, and *Vogue*.

Sánchez Herrero has a Bachelor's in business administration from the Universidad Pontificia Comillas and in luxury management and business from LUISS Business school. She is currently enrolled in a product development program at MIT Sloan and a BFA program in interior architecture and design at The Academy of Art University in San Francisco. Sánchez Herrero resides in Miami, Florida.

Ana Sánchez-Gal, the co-founder and CEO of Oliver Gal, is a distinguished artist, entrepreneur and leader. She launched her first company AllPopArt in 2003 from her apartment, with an idea scribbled on a restaurant napkin and the expenses charged to a credit card. With Sánchez-Gal's entrepreneurial acumen and creative intuition, AllPopArt exploded into a national success and became the parent company to her other brands.

When Sánchez-Gal founded Oliver Gal with her sister Lola, they quickly grew the company from a start-up into an internationally recognized name complete with award-winning, high-impact pop art that has been featured in publications worldwide.

In addition to AllPopArt and Oliver Gal, Sánchez-Gal has developed a robust portfolio of successful brands, including Hatcher & Ethan, Wynwood Studio and the Comics Factory. She received a Bachelor's in business administration from the Universidad Autónoma de Madrid, an Associate's in multimedia and web design from the Art Institute of Fort Lauderdale, and has completed the Executive Education Program in finance at the Wharton School of the University of Pennsylvania. She is currently enrolled in Harvard Business School's Owner/President Management Program.

THANKS

We want to thank Max Ulanoff from Buchwald and Associates for being a true rock star, for believing in us, and always pushing us to uncover new mediums to spread our magic. Meeting you and working together has been an incredible journey so far. We can't wait to see what else we will do together!

To our publisher, Rage Kindelsperger, thank you for being patient, kind, and seeing the potential in our work. It is an honor to have our book included to the list of the beautiful and successful array of books that you have published.

To our editor, Keyla Pizarro-Hernández, who has guided us carefully and ever so patiently throughout writing our first book, we will always hold you in our hearts. When you shared the book pitch and the ideas you had for its flow and composition, you changed our lives and showed us we could walk even further than we ever thought. Thank you.

To Creative Director, Laura Drew, you are a happy ray of sunshine and a thunderbolt in the design world. Thank you for teaching, guiding, helping, and most of all working to preserve the essence of Oliver Gal throughout the book. Thank you for turning our art into a beautiful cover and guiding us through the process of illustrating our words and adding our art to the inspiring stories that this book contains.

Thank you to each of the women that dedicated their time and shared their thoughts with us to be a part of this book. You took the time to come up with the best advice you would give another woman and gave us a piece of knowledge that could inspire anyone to be, do, and feel better. You made a difference to us and to every person holding this book in their hands, perusing through its pages looking for inspiration.

Thank you to the Oliver Gal team, you are our why and our motivation. We hope this book brings you pride and happiness to know that you are part of something bigger. It is because of you that this was possible.

Thanks to Maria Brown and Tyler Travis for helping to coordinate, source the quotes, keep us in schedule when possible and being awesome all around.

To everyone in our family. Thank you for supporting us during this task. Writing a book is a daunting task but knowing that you have our backs makes everything so much better.

Brimming with creative inspiration, how-to projects, and useful information to enrich your everyday life, Quarto Knows is a favorite destination for those pursuing their interests and passions. Visit our site and dig deeper with our books into your area of interest: Quarto Creates, Quarto Cooks, Quarto Homes, Quarto Lives, Quarto Drives, Quarto Explores, Quarto Gifts, or Quarto Kids.

First published in 2020 by Rock Point, an imprint of The Quarto Group, 142 West 36th Street, 4th Floor, New York, NY 10018, USA
T (212) 779-4972 F (212) 779-6058 www.QuartoKnows.com

Rock Point titles are also available at discount for retail, wholesale, promotional and bulk purchase. For details, contact the Special Sales Manager by email at specialsales@quarto.com or by mail at The Quarto Group, Attn: Special Sales Manager, 100 Cummings Center Suite, 265D, Beverly, MA 01915, USA.

10 9 8 7 6 5 4 3 2 1

ISBN: 978-1-63106-708-2

Printed in China

Library of Congress Cataloging-in-Publication Data

Names: Herrero, Lola Sánchez, author. | Gal, Ana Sánchez, author.
Title: Hello gorgeous : empowering quotes from bold women for aspirational
     thinkers / Lola Sánchez Herrero & Ana Sánchez-Gal, CO-Founders of the
     Oliver Gal Artist CO.
Description: New York : Rock Point, 2020. | Series: Everyday inspiration |
     Summary: "Hello Gorgeous is a beautiful gift book filled with empowering
     quotes and motivational anecdotes by powerful women to inspire every
     moment of your courageous life"-- Provided by publisher.
Identifiers: LCCN 2020022913 (print) | LCCN 2020022914 (ebook) | ISBN
     9781631067082 (hardcover) | ISBN 9780760367896 (ebook)
Subjects: LCSH: Motivation (Psychology) | Inspiration. | Self-actualization
     (Psychology)
Classification: LCC BF503 .H455 2020 (print) | LCC BF503 (ebook) | DDC
     155.3/339--dc23
LC record available at https://lccn.loc.gov/2020022913
LC ebook record available at https://lccn.loc.gov/2020022914

Publisher: Rage Kindelsperger
Creative Director: Laura Drew
Managing Editor: Cara Donaldson
Editor: Keyla Pizarro-Hernández
Cover and Interior Design: Lola Sánchez Herrero

ALSO AVAILABLE:

ISBN: 978-1-63106-310-7

ISBN: 978-1-63106-530-9

ISBN: 978-1-63106-641-2